# "All Cut to Pieces and Gone to Hell"

# "All Cut to Pieces and Gone to Hell"

## The Civil War, Race Relations, and the Battle of Poison Spring

edited by Mark K. Christ

August House Publishers, Inc.
LITTLE ROCK

Published 2003 by August House Publishers, Inc.
P.O. Box 3223, Little Rock, Arkansas 72203
501-372-5450
http://www.augusthouse.com

MID-CONTINENT PUBLIC LIBRARY

3 0000 12481753 1

Published in cooperation with
The Butler Center for Arkansas Studies,
Central Arkansas Library System
100 Rock Street, Little Rock, Arkansas 72201.

Printed in the United States of America

10 9 8 7 6 5 4 3 2 1   HB
10 9 8 7 6 5 4 3 2 1   PB

Library of Congress Cataloging-in-Publication Data

"All cut to pieces and gone to hell": the Civil War, race relations, and the Battle of
   Poison Spring / edited by Mark K. Christ.
      p. cm.
   Includes bibliographical references and index.
   ISBN 0-87483-736-7 (alk. paper)—ISBN 0-87483-737-5 (pbk. : alk. paper)
      1. Camden Expedition (1864) 2. Poison Spring, Battle of, Ark., 1864. 3.
   Massacres—Arkansas—History—19th century. 4. African American soldiers—
   Crimes against—Arkansas—History—19th century. 5. Arkansas—Race rela-
   tions. 6. Arkansas—History—Civil War, 1861-1865—Atrocities. 7. United
   States—History—Civil War, 1861-1865—Atrocities. 8. Arkansas—History—
   Civil War, 1861-1865—African Americans. 9. United States—History—Civil
   War, 1861-1865—African Americans. 10. United States—History—Civil War,
   1861-1865—Participation, African American. I.
   Christ, Mark K.

E476.35.A44 2003
973.7'36--dc21

                                                            2003056277

The paper used in this publication meets the minimum requirements of the
American National Standard for Information Sciences—Permanence of Paper for
Printed Library Materials, ANSI Z39.48-1984.

AUGUST HOUSE                    PUBLISHERS                    LITTLE ROCK

To Corporal Jacob Edwards, Company A, First
Kansas Colored Volunteer Infantry, and Private
George May, Company A, Newton's Tenth Cavalry,
Trader's Arkansas Cavalry Battalion, and the other
dead of Poison Spring. May they rest in peace and
may we learn from their sacrifice.

≈

# Acknowledgments

The seminar "'I Have Seen Enough Myself ...': The Battle of Poison Spring," as well as this publication, were made possible by the Old State House Museum, a division of the Department of Arkansas Heritage. Bill Gatewood, Georganne Sisco, Gerry Soltz, Larry Ahart, Gail Moore, and Joellen Maack were key players in bringing the seminar together. Thanks are also due to Tom Dillard, Don Wolfe, Tim Nutt, and Brian K. Robertson of the Central Arkansas Library System's Butler Center for Arkansas Studies. Tom Dillard and CALS director Bobby Roberts read and edited the original manuscript. Holly Hope of the Arkansas Historic Preservation Program provided advice on strengthening aspects of the manuscript. Jody McNeese Keene, H.K. Stewart, Liz Parkhurst, Cindy McFarlane, and the August House staff crafted the manuscript and photographic images into the finished book you see now.

≈

# Contents

# *Introduction*

In 1998, the Old State House Museum in Little Rock acquired a collection of letters associated with the Spence family of Arkadelphia. Alexander E. Spence of Company B, First Arkansas Infantry Regiment, and Thomas F. Spence of Company E, Second Arkansas Mounted Rifles, wrote the majority of them. These letters were the basis for a major exhibit, "Brothers in Arms: The Spence Family and the Civil War," that ran at the Old State House from May 2001 through January 2003.

In addition to the letters from Tom and Alex Spence, the Spence Family Collection also included ten other letters, most written by various friends and comrades of the Spence brothers. One letter, however, did not fit within the general context of the rest of the collection, which focused primarily on activities of the Army of Tennessee east of the Mississippi River. This letter, written on faded blue paper, offers insights into one of the most tragic, savage, and controversial battles that took place in Arkansas: the April 18, 1864, Battle of Poison Spring.

This letter, the signature on which was torn away, did not appear in the exhibit, in part because it did not fit the flow of the stories of Tom and Alex Spence, and in part because of concerns that it would overshadow their experiences. Instead, the letter became the focal point of a one-day seminar held January 26, 2002, at the Old State House. This event, "I Have Seen Enough Myself …: The Battle of Poison Spring Seminar," attracted more than 120 people who learned about the battle, the racial and social revolutions taking place during the Civil War, and the letter itself.

Dr. Thomas A. DeBlack of Arkansas Tech University in Russellville provided an overview of the 1864 Camden Expedition, a Union invasion of south Arkansas in which the Poison Spring battle was fought. Historian Ronnie Nichols discussed the changing role of African-Americans in the Civil War, from slave laborer to fighting man. Dr. Carl Moneyhon of the University of Arkansas at Little Rock explored changes in Southern society as white Southerners dealt with changes in the status of their erstwhile slaves. Frank Arey of the Department of Arkansas Heritage told of the Battle of Honey Springs, Oklahoma, in which many of the future combatants at Poison Spring first fought each other. Mark Christ, guest curator of the "Brothers in Arms" exhibit, discussed the Poison Spring letter and his thoughts on its probable author. And Dr. Gregory J.W. Urwin of Temple University in Philadelphia spoke about racial atrocities that claimed both Union and Confederate victims before the Camden Expedition's end. Versions of all of those addresses are included in this volume.

The Battle of Poison Spring and its bloody aftermath remain a source of great controversy among students of Civil War Arkansas, with some seeing it as a massacre spurred by racial animosity and others viewing it as a continuation of a war that had grown increasingly savage, especially in the Trans-Mississippi South. The Old State House symposium provided a forum for discussion of the issues surrounding Poison Spring— and perhaps underscored the continued need to talk about all aspects of our shared heritage as Arkansans.

—Mark K. Christ
April 15, 2002

# An Overview of the Camden Expedition

## Thomas A. DeBlack

By the winter of 1863–1864 the prospects for a Confederate victory in the American Civil War were growing increasingly slim. Defeat at Gettysburg, Pennsylvania, and the loss of the Mississippi River strongholds of Vicksburg and Port Hudson in 1863 (and with them the loss of control of the Mississippi River itself) had been devastating setbacks. To compound the problem, after long months of disappointment and failure, the Union had by 1864 finally succeeded in putting three of its best generals—Ulysses S. Grant, William Tecumseh Sherman, and Phil Sheridan—in top commands. In addition, the North now fielded an army that outnumbered Southern forces by two to one, and that army was probably the best-supplied and best-equipped army in the world. With the Emancipation Proclamation, any real hope of European intervention on the side of the Confederacy had all but vanished.

In Arkansas during that bitterly cold winter, the Confederate situation was, if anything, even worse than elsewhere. Beginning in March 1862, Federal forces had run off an impressive string of victories—Pea Ridge, Hill's Plantation, Prairie Grove, Arkansas Post, and Fayetteville. Union forces had seized Helena and Pine Bluff and beaten back Confederate attempts to retake the towns. They had also taken Fort Smith and, in early September 1863, captured the capital city of Little Rock. Rebel cavalry had raided Missouri but had been quickly expelled with heavy losses. By the end of 1863, Arkansas Confederates had been driven back to the southwest corner of the state. It appeared that 1864 would be no better. Early in that year a convention of Arkansas Unionists drafted a new state constitution and chose a provisional governor. In March, loyalist voters ratified the charter and formally elected the new governor.[1]

That same month Ulysses Grant was promoted to the rank of lieutenant general and given the title of general in chief of all Federal armies. He moved east to make his headquarters with the Army of the Potomac, but he did not limit his attention to the Virginia theater of operations. Grant believed that for too long the various Union armies had acted without coordination. They were, he noted, "like a balky team, no two ever pulling together."[2]

To remedy this situation, he planned a series of coordinated attacks on several fronts to prevent the Confederate armies from reinforcing one another. George Meade would lead the Army of the Potomac against Robert E. Lee's Army of Northern Virginia; Sherman would move against Joe Johnston and drive deep into the interior of the Confederacy, destroying the South's resources as he went; and three smaller Federal armies would also be brought into play in the hope of stretching Confederate defenses to the breaking point. Benjamin Butler's Army of the James would advance up the Virginia peninsula, cut the railroad between Petersburg and Richmond, and threaten the Confederate capital from the south; Franz Sigel's forces would move up the Shenandoah Valley and cut off Lee's army from that region; and finally, Nathaniel Banks's Army of the Gulf (in Louisiana) would capture Mobile, then move northward to prevent Rebel forces in Alabama from reinforcing Joe Johnston. (President Abraham Lincoln described it as, "Those not skinning can hold a leg.") The attacks were set to commence in May 1864.[3]

But before it could take part in Grant's grand design, one Federal army had other business to attend to. Grant's predecessor, Henry Halleck, had, with Lincoln's approval, ordered Nathaniel Banks to move on Shreveport via the Red River, then into east Texas. The move would extend Union control into northwest Louisiana and east Texas, and the cotton seized from the surrounding region would swell the Federal treasury and supply the needs of idle New England textile mills. The Federal presence in the region would also end any possible alliance between Confederate forces and those of Napoleon III's French forces in Mexico. To accomplish his task, Banks would be loaned ten thousand troops from Sherman's command; he also would be supported in his movement up the Red by naval forces under the command of Rear Admiral David D. Porter. A second Federal force led by Major General Frederick Steele would move south from Little Rock and link up with Banks's army at Shreveport. The operation would be styled the Red River Expedition.[4]

No man has been more closely associated with the story of the Red River Expedition than Nathaniel Banks. A Massachusetts native and the son of a cotton mill worker, Banks had himself worked in the mills as a child. A self-taught man, he had risen rapidly through the political ranks, first in the Massachusetts legislature and later in the national Congress. By 1856, he was speaker of the U.S. House of Representatives. The following year, he was elected governor of Massachusetts. He left office in 1860 to become vice president of the Illinois Central Railroad, succeeding George B. McClellan. When the Civil War began, he returned to Massachusetts. Banks had no military experience, but he was a prominent antislavery Republican from an important Northern state, and Abraham Lincoln could not afford to ignore him. He was commissioned a major general and sent to Maryland, thus becoming, as one historian noted, "the quintessential political general—politically connected but militarily incompetent."[5]

While Banks looked every bit the soldier, he proved to be an ineffective commander. In the spring of 1862 he was soundly drubbed by Stonewall Jackson in a series of battles in the Shenandoah Valley and had so great a quantity of his supplies captured by Jackson's forces that the Confederates derisively referred to him as "Commissary Banks." After being bested by Jackson again in the Second Bull Run Campaign, he was transferred to New Orleans in November 1862. (Students of the Confederate effort in the Trans-Mississippi will recognize this tactic.) He did succeed in capturing Port Hudson on July 8, 1863, though he suffered four thousand casualties, lost another seven thousand men to disease, and nearly caused the destruction of a Union fleet in the process.[6]

Banks's cohort in the Red River Expedition was Frederick Steele. A West Point graduate (class of 1843, where he graduated thirtieth, nine places behind classmate Ulysses Grant), Steele had led a battalion at the Battle of Wilson's Creek, Missouri, on August 10, 1861; had participated in the capture of Helena in July 1862; and had served under William Tecumseh Sherman at the battles of Chickasaw Bluffs and Arkansas Post. He was promoted to major general and led a division throughout the Vicksburg campaign. After Vicksburg's fall, Steele returned to Helena and assumed command of all Union forces in Arkansas at the end of July 1863.[7]

In August 1863 he set out with twelve thousand men to capture Little Rock. The city fell on September 10 after a campaign that lasted one month and cost Steele only 137 casualties. The ease with which he had taken the capital city convinced Steele that organized Confederate resistance in Arkansas was almost at an end.[8]

Despite his success, Steele was not particularly popular among his own troops, many of whom disapproved of his lenient treatment of Confederate civilians. Behind his back, some called him a Copperhead, a term for Northern Democrats who opposed the Lincoln administration and the war. Under Steele's occupation, Little Rock experienced an economic revival. It was one of the few towns that occupying Federal soldiers in Arkansas liked. (By contrast, they called Helena "Hell in Arkansas.") In fact, they liked it so much that many were reluctant to leave. Their journeys through the state had convinced them that this was the most civilized—and probably the safest—place in Arkansas.[9]

The amenities of Little Rock were not the only reason that Frederick Steele was dismayed when he received orders to march his army southwest across Arkansas to Shreveport. Steele reminded Halleck that his proposed route of march was over bad roads through a region almost destitute of provisions, and he feared increased guerrilla activity and a renewed threat to his supply lines if he left Little Rock. His objections were overruled, however, and on March 23, 1864, he set out as the northern wing of the Red River Expedition. Though Camden originally had nothing to do with the plan, the Arkansas phase of the operation would afterwards be known as the Camden Expedition.[10]

Steele was to leave Little Rock with eighty-five hundred men. At Arkadelphia, seventy miles to the southwest, he would be joined by four thousand men of the Frontier Division led by Brigadier General John M. Thayer, who was moving southeast from Fort Smith. Muddy roads slowed the progress of Steele's army as it marched through Benton and on to the largely deserted village of Rockport, where it crossed the Ouachita River. Steele reached Arkadelphia on March 29, but there was no sign of Thayer. He waited for three days while his troops consumed valuable rations and sacked a female seminary. Then, on April 1, he continued on southwestward, still without Thayer's troops.[11]

While the Yankees moved southward, the bulk of the Confederate army remained at Camden. Command of Confederate forces in the state had passed from the chronically ill and prematurely infirm Theophilus Holmes to Sterling Price. Price, whom one historian has dubbed "the central figure in the Civil War west of the Mississippi," had been a prosperous Missouri tobacco planter before the war. He had also served as a state legislator and a U.S. congressman, been a colonel in the Mexican War, and, after a brief interlude, was governor of Missouri from 1853 to 1857. Price had been victorious at Wilson's Creek in 1861 but was soon driven out of Missouri. A generation older than many of the soldiers under his command, Price quickly became "Old Pap" to his troops and was one of the most widely loved and respected leaders on either side during the first three years of the war.[12]

Price's orders from Edmund Kirby Smith, the supreme Confederate commander in the Trans-Mississippi, were to prevent Steele from linking up with Banks, but Price's army had been seriously weakened when two of his infantry divisions were ordered to Louisiana to oppose Banks. With only thirty-two hundred cavalrymen, he dared not risk a formal battle with the much larger Federal force. Instead he sent detachments of his cavalry under John Marmaduke and Jo Shelby to harass the front and rear of Steele's column.[13]

John Sappington Marmaduke, the son of a prominent Missouri family, had studied at Harvard and Yale before graduating from West Point in 1857. Beginning the war as a colonel in the Missouri militia, he fought at Shiloh, Tennessee, and Prairie Grove, Arkansas. As the year 1863 began, the twenty-nine-year-old Marmaduke had already advanced to the rank of brigadier general. Still, by 1864 his most famous accomplishment may have been the killing of another Confederate general in a duel in September 1863.[14]

Joseph Orville "Jo" Shelby, the scion of a prominent Kentucky family, had moved to Missouri in the early 1850s and had run a hemp business before the war. A slaveowner and a Confederate sympathizer, he was involved in the war from its inception, first as a "border ruffian" in "Bleeding Kansas" and later with Missouri state troops at Wilson's Creek and Pea Ridge.[15]

Shelby was hailed by some on both sides as one of the best cavalry commanders in the war. His reputation was greatly enhanced by the writings of his adjutant, John Edwards, a former newspaperman with a love of the bottle and a flair for the dramatic, who idolized his commander. It was Edwards who wrote most of Shelby's after-action reports, and in these (as in three books he wrote in later years) he made Shelby a larger-than-life figure. Even allowing for Edwards's exaggeration and prevarication, it is possible to argue that few other figures on either side played a more prominent role in the Civil War in Arkansas than did Jo Shelby. Before the war ended, he would fight in almost every major engagement in the state, and he was a constant thorn in the side of Federal forces in Arkansas.[16]

On April 3, the Federals reached the north bank of the Little Missouri River at Elkin's Ferry. With his supplies rapidly dwindling and his men on half rations, Steele hoped to move to Camden on the Ouachita River where he could be resupplied. (Shreveport was forgotten. Shelby Foote has remarked that it might as well have been on "the back side of the moon.") But Camden was strongly fortified and occupied by the main body of Price's army. Steele pressed on southwestward without Thayer, hoping that by moving toward the Confederate state capital at Washington he could draw Price out of Camden.[17]

Steele left a brigade of infantry at Okolona, about five miles from Elkin's Ferry, to protect his rear and watch for Thayer's column. Around nine in the morning, Shelby's Rebel cavalry struck the isolated Federal rear guard, and a fierce three-hour fight ensued. In the midst of the battle, a tremendous hailstorm moved in from the northeast, transforming the battlefield into a surrealistic landscape. Shelby's after-action report noted, "The scene was rugged and sublime. Amid the jar of the thunder, the flash of the lightning, and the moaning and sighing of the pines as the pitiless hail-storm tore through them, there was mingled the crash of artillery, the sharp rattle of musketry, and ever and anon as the wind ceased there came the wild blare of bugles and the ring of sabers."[18] What was surely one of the most bizarre engagements of the war ended when Federal artillery upset a large number of beehives, and the swarming bees forced the Rebels to withdraw.[19]

Later in the day Marmaduke unsuccessfully assaulted the main Federal column along the banks of the Little Missouri. Repulsed, he struck again at six

*Brigadier General John S. Marmaduke was acting Confederate commander in the attack on the Union foraging expedition at Poison Spring. (Courtesy of the Library of Congress)*

o'clock the next morning, hitting the Federals as they were crossing the Little Missouri River. After five hours of fighting, the Rebels withdrew sixteen miles to the south and took up positions at Prairie D'Ane (near present-day Prescott) between the Yankees and Washington. Despite the fierce fighting, casualties were light.[20]

On April 5, Steele moved to meet the Rebels but halted when word reached him that Thayer's division was just a few days march away. Convinced that Steele's objective was the Confederate capital, Price moved the remainder of the Confederate garrison out of Camden and joined Marmaduke and Shelby at Prairie D'Ane on April 7. His force was bolstered by the arrival of two mounted brigades from the Indian Territory—the Twenty-ninth Texas Cavalry and a Choctaw brigade led by Colonel Tandy Walker—numbering about fifteen hundred men.[21]

On April 9, Thayer's Frontier Division finally caught up with Steele's main body. It included the First and Second Kansas Colored Volunteers, regiments composed largely of former slaves from Arkansas and Missouri under the command of white officers. Thayer's arrival brought Steele's total strength to about fifteen thousand men, but the new arrivals brought few, if any, supplies. With his troops already on half rations, Steele sent an urgent message to Little Rock requesting thirty days' half rations for fifteen thousand men, then pressed on toward the Rebels at Prairie D'Ane.[22]

The following day Steele's columns moved to within a mile of the Confederate entrenchments, where they stopped and threw up earthworks of their own. Sporadic artillery duels and skirmishing, punctuated by long periods of inactivity, occupied the next two days. By nightfall on April 10, the lines were close enough for the opposing pickets to taunt one another.[23]

In fact, neither army seemed eager to confront the other. Finally, on April 12, Steele moved in force against the Confederate lines, but the Rebels were no longer there. Price had withdrawn to within eight miles of Washington. Steele, undoubtedly relieved, turned his army to the east and made for Camden, some forty miles away. Price took up pursuit, and Rebel cavalry again slashed at the front and rear of the Federal column, but the Yankees reached the safety of Camden's fortifications on April 15.[24]

Steele was not out of the woods yet, however, and he knew it. His troops were exhausted by the march across swollen streams, through heavy rain and seemingly bottomless mud, and his supplies were desperately low. The army had been forced to forage from five to fifteen miles on either side of its line of march to find fodder for the horses and mules and food for the men. Despite the heavy rains, drinking water was also in short supply because Confederate guerrillas had dumped animal carcasses in many local wells.[25]

Some Arkansas civilians interpreted the move to Camden as a retreat. One area resident noted in her diary, "Our cavalry are fighting Steele near Washington. Report says Steele is slowly retreating toward Camden with Shelby and Marmaduke hanging like hungry wolves along his line."[26] The Rebels, outnumbered two to one, could not attack Camden directly, but their cavalry watched the roads leading from the town for Federal patrols or foraging parties.[27]

After some initial looting by Federal soldiers, Steele succeeded in restraining his men from pillaging local civilians, and, as he had done in Little Rock, established a good relationship with the townspeople. When supplies did not arrive by April 17, Steele was forced to act. Word had reached his quartermaster of the existence of five thousand bushels of corn sixteen miles west of town. Steele promptly dispatched 198 wagons to seize the corn and other supplies. The wagons were escorted by 1,170 men (821 infantry, 291 cavalry, 58 artillery) and four cannon from Thayer's Frontier Division, including 438 officers and men from the First Kansas Colored Infantry.[28]

Rebel forces managed to destroy about half the supply of corn before the Federals arrived, but the Yankees seized the remainder. At sunrise the next morning, April 18, the loaded wagon train began the return trip to Camden. The column had gone about five miles when it ran into trouble. Alerted by their patrols, about thirty-six hundred Confederate cavalry, backed by twelve cannon, took a position

Colonel James Monroe Williams led the First Kansas Colored Infantry and commanded the Union forces at Poison Spring. (Courtesy of the Gregory J.W. Urwin Collection)

between the returning supply train and Camden along high ground at Poison Spring, fourteen miles west of the town. The senior Confederate officer on the field was Brigadier General Samuel B. Maxey, but Maxey turned battlefield command over to Marmaduke, who had come up with the plan to intercept the Federal train. Marmaduke's command consisted of Arkansas, Missouri, and Texas troops and a Choctaw brigade from the Indian Territory. They would fight dismounted using long-range infantry rifles.[29]

When the Confederates opened fire on the Federals' advance guard, Union commander James M. Williams formed his troops into an L-shaped defensive position around the wagons with the First Kansas Colored in the center, the Eighteenth Iowa on their left, and the cavalry on the flanks. The First Kansas Colored bore the brunt of the assault. They repelled two attacks but suffered heavy casualties. A third Rebel charge broke the Union line and drove the Yankees back through the wagons. The entire position soon collapsed. The Rebels overran the wagon train and pursued the fleeing blue-coats. One Rebel colonel recalled, "Away trotted the poor black men into the forest clinging to their rifles, but not using them, while the pursuing Confederates cut them down right and left."

Williams rallied a portion of his command in a swamp north of the battlefield, but the Rebels made no further pursuit, and the remainder of the Union force retreated north and east in a wide arc toward the safety of Camden. The first of them reached the town around eight o'clock that night.[30]

The Rebels captured all the wagons, four cannon, and twelve hundred mules, and inflicted over three hundred casualties while suffering only ninety-five. The Battle of Poison Spring was one of the greatest Confederate successes of the entire war in Arkansas, but it was forever tarnished by the events that followed the initial engagement. Other articles in this volume will address this issue in some detail, but suffice it to say that the First Kansas Colored suffered a disproportionate share of the casualties, particularly in the number of men killed.[31]

For Steele, the debacle at Poison Spring was compounded when a scout brought bad news from Louisiana. On April 8, Confederate Major General Richard Taylor trapped Banks at Sabine Crossroads and soundly defeated him. Banks fell back to Pleasant Hill, where the Rebels struck him again the next day. This time the Yankees held their ground and sent the Rebels reeling backward with heavy losses. But Banks's nerves were shot. He fell back to Grand Ecore, then Alexandria, and then on to New Orleans. His retreat freed thousands of additional Confederate soldiers to concentrate against Steele's embattled command at Camden.[32]

On April 20, a supply train reached Camden from Pine Bluff carrying ten days' worth of provisions. Two days later, Steele sent the 240-wagon train back to Pine Bluff for additional provisions, escorted by more than fourteen hundred troops under the command of Francis M. Drake and accompanied by a large number of civilians and about three hundred former slaves. On April 25, a relief party of 150 cavalry from Pine Bluff rendezvoused with Drake, bringing his total strength to 1,690. As at Poison Spring, the Rebels had been alerted to the Federal train's movement. Three days out of Camden, the Federal column approached a series of grist mills owned by Hastings Marks. Four thousand Confederate cavalry under General James Fagan waited along the road. At eight in the morning, when the Federal advance guard came into view, the Rebels attacked.[33]

One division led by William Cabell struck the wagon train from the southeast. The Federal troops resisted fiercely, and a desperate struggle ensued. As this fighting raged, a second Rebel division led by Jo Shelby attacked along the Camden road from the northeast, striking the left flank and rear of the Federal line and driving the Yankees back. After five hours of intense fighting, the Federal commander, himself wounded in the thigh, surrendered. Remarkably, he had suffered only about a hundred men killed, but the Rebels took thirteen hundred prisoners and seized all the wagons.[34]

Finding few supplies in the wagons, the Confederates went after the survivors. One Federal prisoner reported,

> The rebs robbed nearly every man of us to our Chaplain & many of our dead they stripped of every stitch of clothes even their shirts & socks & left them unburyed & the woods on fire & many of the wounded they jurked off their boots, blouses, pants, and hats.[35]

Again reports surfaced of the murder of blacks. Total Confederate casualties were less than three hundred. A Federal soldier later acknowledged that the little-known Battle of Marks' Mills "was one of the most substantial successes gained by the western Confederates during the war."[36]

For Steele, it was the final straw. With supplies rapidly dwindling and the Confederate forces outside Camden growing, he had no choice but to attempt to get back to Little Rock. The Federals quietly stole out of Camden and crossed the Ouachita River during the night of April 26 and headed north toward the capital, a hundred miles away. It was the chance the Confederates had been waiting for. But for once their cavalry patrols let them down. By the time the Rebels realized that the Federals were gone and began their pursuit, Steele's forces were well on their way.[37]

As they hastened northward, rumors began to spread through the Federal ranks that a Rebel army had worked its way between them and Little Rock. Indeed, on April 27, Fagan's command, moving north from the Marks' Mills battle-field, had crossed the very road along which the Yankees were moving without ever knowing of their presence. The following day, Kirby Smith left Camden with the main body of his army. Before Smith left, however, he made a serious mistake. Informed of reports of an impending Federal invasion of the Indian Territory, he sent Maxey's division back there.[38]

By the afternoon of April 29, the Confederate vanguard caught up with the rear guard of the retreating Federals. In the meantime, however, twenty-two miles north of Princeton, the Federal vanguard reached the rain-swollen Saline River crossing at Jenkins' Ferry (about twelve miles southwest of present-day Sheridan and a little over forty miles from Little Rock). The engineers quickly began construction of a pontoon bridge. By a quarter past three, the bridge was in place and the engineers went to work improving the approach to the bridge. As soon as that job was completed, the Federal vanguard began crossing. By six o'clock they were all east of the Saline, and the wagon train began to cross.[39]

It was a slow process under the best of conditions, and a driving rain made it even more so. The riverbank soon became "a sea of mud." Wagons sank to their axles and mules lost their footing. "The rain came down in torrents," a Federal soldier noted, "the men became exhausted, and both they and the animals sank down in the mud and mire, wherever they were, to seek a few hours' repose." At around nine-twenty in the

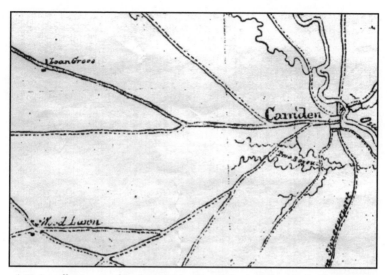

*A Union officer's map of Steele's Camden Expedition includes this detail of the area west of Camden, where the Battle of Poison Spring occurred. (Courtesy of Charles Witsell)*

evening, any further attempts to get the wagons across the bridge were postponed until the next day.[40]

Early the next morning, while the Federal wagon train still stretched back two miles down the road toward Princeton, Kirby Smith arrived with the main body of the pursuing Confederate army and attacked the retreating Yankees in force. Steele had protected the crossing point with rifle pits and breastworks, and his soldiers gave ground grudgingly. The return of Price's two divisions from Louisiana increased Confederate strength to about eight thousand men, but Federal forces benefited from the weather and the terrain of the battlefield. From the point where the attack began, the terrain sloped down to the riverbank, funneling the attacking force into an area only about a quarter-mile across. With a swamp to one side and a hill to the other, flanking movements were impossible, and the Confederates were unable to deploy their entire force at one time. Rain-softened ground slowed the attackers, and smoke and mist obscured much of the field. Time and again the Confederates charged, only to be driven back with heavy losses.[41]

Around half past twelve in the afternoon the exhausted Rebels called off the attack, and by three o'clock the entire Federal army was safely on the north bank of the river. Steele ordered the pontoon bridge destroyed to prevent further pursuit, and the bespattered Federal columns sloshed on toward Little Rock. They reached the capital on May 3, looking, one observer noted, "as if they had been rolled in the mud." The Camden Expedition was the greatest Federal disaster of the Civil War in Arkansas. Union forces lost over twenty-five hundred men killed, wounded, or missing. In addition, hundreds of wagons and thousands of livestock were lost. The Federals had gained not one inch of ground.[42]

The failure of the Federals' Camden expedition breathed new life into moribund Arkansas Confederates. All across the state, emboldened Rebel forces went on the offensive. The threat of a Rebel invasion of north central Arkansas, combined with a shortage of horses and food, forced the Union forces to abandon Batesville and Jacksonport. Several hundred Arkansas Unionists had to be evacuated to Little Rock. Confederate guerrillas raided Federally-leased plantations around Helena, tore up stretches of railroad track between DeVall's Bluff and Little Rock, and harassed Union shipping on the Mississippi River in southeast Arkansas.[43]

It seemed that the Confederate commanders in Arkansas had at last found a formula that might at best win back the state or at least confine Federal influence to Little Rock and a handful of strongly-garrisoned towns. But it was not to be. Sterling Price saw a chance to realize the dream of a triumphant return to Missouri that he had harbored ever since his ignominious retreat from that state in February 1862.[44]

On September 19, 1864, he led twelve thousand men (four thousand of them without weapons and a thousand with no horses) across the Missouri line and headed for St. Louis. Over the course of the next four and a half weeks, he recruited new soldiers, lost others, burned some towns, tore up bridges and railroads, overran several smaller Federal garrisons, threatened—though he did not capture—both St. Louis and the Missouri state capital at Jefferson City, criss-crossed the state from east to west all the way into Kansas, and generally caused such an uproar that Federal authorities dispatched over twenty thousand troops to deal with him. The opposing armies clashed in and around Westport, Missouri, on October 22 and 23 in the largest Civil War battle (in terms of the number of men engaged) fought west of the Mississippi. The Confederates lost at least fifteen hundred men killed and wounded, and another two thousand were taken prisoner.[45]

Price turned his defeated army southward, but ten days later Federal forces caught up with him at Mine Creek in Kansas and inflicted another twelve hundred casualties. By the time he returned to Arkansas on October 30, Price had only four thousand survivors. With this ragged remnant, he moved briefly into the Indian Territory and Texas before returning to southwest Arkansas with thirty-five hundred men, the majority of them unarmed. In a little over two months, Price had squandered the momentum that had been won the previous spring and in the process destroyed the high esteem in which he had been held by many of his troops. "Men are greatly demoralized and we present a pitiable forlorn aspect," one Rebel veteran grumbled. "God damn Old Price."[46]

In late 1864, events on the national political scene were also trending against the Confederacy. On Tuesday, November 8, voters in the North reelected Abraham Lincoln to a second term as president. Lincoln's election dashed any hope in the South for a negotiated peace. With the failure of Price's raid and the reelection of Lincoln, Union forces in Arkansas once again gained the upper hand, but events east of the Mississippi soon robbed them of their advantage. Federal reinforcements were needed in Georgia and the Carolinas, where Sherman relentlessly pursued Confederate forces under Joseph Johnston, and along the Gulf Coast at Mobile.[47]

By early 1865, the antagonists in Arkansas, prevented by lack of numbers from conducting major offensive operations, adopted defensive stances. The Civil War in the state would end not with a bang but with a whimper. For Arkansas Confederates there had been few highlights. For all the grandiose offensive dreams of the Rebel commanders who served there, the Confederacy's greatest success in Arkansas came when it was on the defensive in opposing Steele's Camden Expedition of 1864.

≈

1. For a detailed description of the war in Arkansas, see Mark Christ, ed., *Rugged and Sublime: The Civil War in Arkansas* (Fayetteville: University of Arkansas Press, 1994) and Thomas A. DeBlack, *With Fire and Sword: Arkansas, 1861-1874* (Fayetteville: University of Arkansas Press, 2003).

2. For a detailed description of Grant's strategy and the attempts to implement it, see Shelby Foote, *The Civil War: A Narrative*, vol. 3 (New York: Random House, 1974), 3-145. The quotation is from page 13.

3. Ibid.; the Lincoln quote is from page 23.

4. Ibid., 25-61.

5. Michael J. Connolly, "Nathaniel Prentiss Banks," in David S. Heidler and Jeanne T. Heidler, eds., *Encyclopedia of the American Civil War: A Political, Social, and Military History*, vol. 1 (Santa Barbara, California: ABC-CLIO, 2000), 174-6.

6. Ibid.

7. Gregory J. W. Urwin, "Frederick Steele," *Encyclopedia of the American Civil War*, vol. 4, 1856-7.

8. DeBlack, *With Fire and Sword*, 92-6

9. Ibid.; Urwin, *Encyclopedia of the American Civil War*, 1857.

10. DeBlack, *With Fire and Sword*, 109.

11. Ibid.

12. Buck T. Foster, "Sterling Price," in *Encyclopedia of the American Civil War*, vol. 3, 1562-1563; the quotation is from Albert Castel's excellent book, *General Sterling Price and the Civil War in the West* (Louisiana State University Press, 1968), vii.

13. DeBlack, *With Fire and Sword*, 109.

14. David S. Heidler and Jeanne T. Heidler, "John Sappington Marmaduke," in *Encyclopedia of the American Civil War*, vol. 3, 1254-5.

15. Mark E. Scott, "Joseph Orville Shelby," in *Encyclopedia of the American Civil War*, vol. 4, 1745-6.

16. Ibid.; see also Daniel Sutherland's foreword to the 2000 edition of Daniel O'Flaherty's *General Jo Shelby: Undefeated Rebel* (Chapel Hill: University of North Carolina Press), xiv-xv.

17. DeBlack, *With Fire and Sword*, 109. Foote's quote is from *The Civil War: A Narrative*, vol. 3, 67.

18. *The War of the Rebellion: A Compilation of the Official Records of the Union and Confederate Armies*, 70 vols. (Washington, D.C., 1880-1901), ser. 1, 34, pt. 1: 837-8.

19. DeBlack, *With Fire and Sword*, 109-10.

20. Ibid., 110.

21. Ibid.

22. Ibid., 110-1.

23. Ibid., 111.

24. Ibid.

25. Ibid.; Daniel Sutherland, "1864,' in Christ, ed., *Rugged and Sublime*, 114.

26. Carl H. Moneyhon, ed., "Life in Confederate Arkansas: The Diary of Virginia Davis Gray, 1863-1865, Part I," *Arkansas Historical Quarterly* 42 (Spring 1983).

27. Sutherland, *Rugged and Sublime*, 114.

28. DeBlack, *With Fire and Sword*, 111-2.

29. The best account of the events at Poison Spring is Gregory J.W. Urwin, "'Cut to Pieces and Gone to Hell': The Poison Spring Massacre," in *North and South: The Official Magazine of the Civil War Society*, vol. 3, no. 6, 45-57.

30. Ibid.

31. Ibid.

32. DeBlack, *With Fire and Sword*, 114; R. Blake Dunnavent, "Red River Campaign," in *Encyclopedia of the American Civil War*, vol. 4, 1616.

33. DeBlack, *With Fire and Sword*, 114; Sutherland, *Rugged and Sublime*, 117.

34. DeBlack, *With Fire and Sword*, 114; Sutherland, *Rugged and Sublime*, 117-9.

35. Quoted in Sutherland, *Rugged and Sublime*, 119.

36. DeBlack, *With Fire and Sword*, 114-5.

37. Ibid., 115.

38. For a detailed discussion see Edwin C. Bearrs, *Steele's Retreat from Camden and the Battle of Jenkins' Ferry* (Little Rock: Pioneer Press, 1961).

39. Ibid.

40. Ibid.

41. Ibid.

42. DeBlack, *With Fire and Sword*, 116-7.

43. Ibid., 117.

44. Ibid., 122-3.

45. Ibid., 123-6.

46. Ibid., 126-30.

47. Ibid., 133-6.

# White Society and African-American Soldiers

## Carl H. Moneyhon

The character of military encounters between blacks and whites during the Civil War has produced considerable discussion in a field of study where controversy has never been constrained. Particular attention has been paid to the question of whether or not Confederate soldiers massacred black troops in these engagements; that is, whether or not they killed men who had ceased resistance. No single incident has attracted more attention than that at Fort Pillow, Tennessee, at least in part because it produced a contemporary congressional investigation. There were many other cases, however, where Union officials charged Confederates with such atrocities, including Poison Spring, Arkansas. In recent years the developing scholarly consensus has been that massacres did take place, especially at Fort Pillow. On the other hand, many students of the Civil War do not accept that conclusion.

This essay seeks to contribute to our understanding of the character of black-white encounters during the Civil War. It does not ask what happened in any specific incident, however, but rather what was possible. Rather than examining the evidence concerning any specific incident, it explores the mind of white Southerners to discover how they would have perceived battle with their former slaves and what actions they would have considered appropriate. In short, it asks if the killing of men who had ceased to fight was a possibility given the world view of Confederate soldiers.

*The July 4, 1863, issue of* Harper's Weekly *showed black troops involved in fighting at Milliken's Bend in Louisiana. After-battle reports included allegations that African-American soldiers were killed after being captured. (Courtesy of the Butler Center for Arkansas Studies, Central Arkansas Library System, Little Rock)*

At the time of the outbreak of the American Civil War, the relationship of white Southerners with African-American slaves was one that historian Leon Litwack has aptly described as being "riddled with ambiguity."[1] The indistinct character of the relationship was based on assumptions by whites about blacks as a race that were inherently contradictory. On the one hand, whites viewed their black slaves as possessing racial traits that uniquely suited them for bondage. Whites described blacks as submissive, light-hearted, amiable, ingratiating, imitative, simple, and irresponsible, all reflecting a racial inferiority that suited them for bondage. On the other hand, whites also saw blacks as possessing darker traits including potential treachery, anger, and even violence. The presence of the latter characteristics indicated a people who would not be content with servitude. The two points of view did not coincide well and required some rationalization.

Whites reconciled the apparent contradictions with explanations that changed over time. In the seventeenth and eighteenth centuries, most whites probably considered blacks barely human, if they thought about them at all, and saw their traits as similar to those of animals. By the nineteenth century, the familiarity of whites with blacks for nearly two hundred years had undermined any real belief that blacks were not human and a new explanation had emerged. The inconsistencies in white attitudes towards slaves were explained away by defining blacks as being at a stage of development similar to a child's. The slave was human, but child-like. Like the child, the slave was dominated by animal instincts. Also as in the case of the child, others had to teach the discipline necessary to suppress these animal instincts. In this way the individual became socialized.

White Southerners believed, however, that the slave was different from the child because, as a race, blacks could never progress beyond this undisciplined, childish stage. To keep blacks socialized, whites had to maintain unstinting discipline. Ultimately, this justified slavery and established the natural relationship between white and black. One of the best-known affirmations of this during the Civil War is that of Vice President Alexander Stephens in his famous "Corner Stone Speech." Discussing the new Confederacy and the South, he asserted that the new government rejected the "assumption of the equality of races. This was an error." Instead, the new government's cornerstone rested "upon the great truth, that the negro is not equal to the white man; that slavery, subordination to the superior race, is his natural and normal condition."[2] A less well-known Southerner, a plantation mistress from North Carolina, would put it even more succinctly: "Freedom for whites, slavery for negroes, God has so ordained it!"[3]

The relationship based upon the assumption of the infantile nature of blacks that whites built with their slaves has been called "paternalism" by historians.[4] The concept of paternalism came out of medieval Europe and implied a reciprocal relationship in which each party had mutual duties and responsibilities towards one another. In the case of the prewar South, slaves worked faithfully for their masters and provided the master with the product of their labor. Their masters, in turn, offered protection and provided an ordered world in which slaves could act in a civilized manner and fulfill basic material and intellectual needs. In short, slaves worked and masters exercised power. A critical part of this view of mutual responsibility was the master's belief that among his responsibilities was that of ensuring the discipline of the slave. Like the father who punished the "bad child," the master punished the "bad slave." Like the contemporary father, the master did not hesitate to resort to physical force to maintain order.

Prior to the Civil War, this system created a world in which most slaves were under control, or at least seldom showed open disobedience to a master. This allowed whites to conclude that when under proper supervision, African-Americans, as a race, were docile and obedient. In retrospect, the fact that open disobedience was rare is not surprising. The price of insubordination was too high. The simplest defiance of authority, even a look, could result in losses of privilege, the movement of a house servant to the fields, or a whipping. The severity of whippings increased if the slave proved intractable. Ultimately, slaves who proved to be hard cases usually were sold to another master who had a reputation for controlling slaves. Within this world, the slave who touched the master, who was violent against whites, or, in the worst possible scenario, rose up in rebellion, faced the ultimate penalty—death.

Nonetheless, most whites did not see black behavior as reflecting a rational response to the situation. They saw it as reflecting the African-American slave's particular character type, one which proved tractable if controlled. Ironically, whites believed that the slave's submission to the master's authority created a bond between the two in which the servant developed loyalty towards the master. Given this perception, it is not surprising that while white Southerners always saw their slaves as potentially dangerous, they generally never believed that the slave population presented any danger to the white people of the South.

When the war began most whites continued to express their belief that their slaves would not be a problem. Many whites maintained this view up to the war's end. As long as slaves were under control, they would behave well and remain loyal to their masters. Such slaves gave their masters little reason for distrust and remained subservient and loyal.

*Lieutenant General E. Kirby Smith, on learning that black soldiers had been taken prisoner at Milliken's Bend, wrote to a fellow officer: "I hope this may not be so, and that your subordinates...may have recognized the propriety of giving no quarter to Negroes and their officers." (Courtesy of the Old State House Museum)*

The reasons for this behavior were complex. Some slaves clearly had come to consider themselves to be part of the family of the master. A slave of the Lipscomb family of South Carolina would later remember her anger at the destruction of the young men of the family. "I so mad," she told an interviewer, "I could have kilt all de Yankees. I say I be happy iffen I could kill me jes' one Yankee. I hated dem 'cause dey hurt my white people."[5] Another South Carolina slave made it his responsibility to protect the property of his master's family. This slave sewed up the family silver into his mattress and slept on it every night to protect it. When Federal raiders arrived at the plantation, the servant refused to tell them where he had hidden the family's property.[6]

White Southerners reacted with great satisfaction both privately and publicly when their slaves did remain loyal, no matter what promoted that loyalty. Typical of these expressions was Edmund Ruffin's, when he observed that the slaves in Virginia had given no indication of anything but faithfulness. "It may be truly said," he wrote, "that every house & family is every night perfectly exposed to any attempt of our slaves to commit robbery or murder. Yet we all feel so secure, & are so free from all suspicion of such danger, that no care is taken for self-protection & in many cases, as in mine, not even the outer door is locked."[7] A Mississippi newspaper expressed equal self-assurance when the first subscriber to the Confederate war loan in Port Gibson, Mississippi, was a slave. The editor wrote: "The feeling at the South can be learned from this little incident. The negroes are ready to fight for their people, and they are ready to give money as well as their lives to the cause of their masters."[8] Ultimately, these "good slaves" would become the stuff of legend in the postwar South.

Such self-congratulation rings hollow given overall circumstances, however. In fact, the whole view of slavery adopted by whites before the war was under attack almost from its beginning. White views about slavery and their slaves necessarily responded, changing and adapting to explain new circumstances. Most whites early on became aware that everything was not as it seemed. Mary Chesnut of South Carolina expressed a growing uncertainty about her slaves when she observed their reactions to the firing on Fort Sumter in April, 1861. She was certain that they were aware that their future was involved in what was happening, that a Southern defeat meant their freedom. She could find no inkling of that realization in their behavior, however. "Not by one word or look can we detect any change in the demeanor of these Negro servants," she wrote. "Lawrence sits at our door, as sleepy and as respectful and as profoundly indifferent. So are they all." Chesnut wondered, however, if their behavior reflected true indifference. She did not believe it was possible for them to be totally unaware of the significance of events. Rather than providing comfort, their behavior caused Chesnut to wonder whether she really knew her slaves at all and ultimately to speculate on their loyalty. "Are they stolidly stupid," she wrote in her diary, "or wiser than we are, silent and strong, biding their time."[9]

Chesnut's early concerns spread rapidly among other white Southerners and the need for speculation concerning slaves' knowledge of circumstances and their response to it quickly became unnecessary. Masters across the South became aware that their slaves knew all too well what the war signified for them. They also found slaves willing to take advantage of whatever opportunity that the war presented to change their individual circumstances. Their challenges to slavery varied, however, because across the South the factors creating opportunity for rebellion differed. On some plantations it was simply the absence of a master or overseer capable of maintaining control. Elsewhere the flight of masters or the presence of Federal soldiers opened up other possibilities. Overall though, most slaves did not remain "good" slaves.

Whites had no alternative but to adapt their views of slavery and race to these new circumstances. These changing ideas provide the cultural and ideological framework within which Confederate citizens and soldiers would deal with blacks. Ultimately, they created the psychology within which Confederate soldiers would respond to black troops.

Understanding how white attitudes changed requires some understanding of how the slaves responded to the war and what this provoked in the development of white ideas. Sometimes what happened was subtle, at other times it was quite drastic. The most common perceived change was a growing insolence and signs of disrespect among slaves. Betty Maury of Fredericksburg, Virginia, observed in April 1862 that many slaves in that area were "beginning to be very independent and impudent."[10] The editor of the Selma, Alabama, *Morning Reporter* complained in August 1863 that the war and the withdrawal of many men into the army had led the Negroes to "becoming so saucy and abusive that a police force has become positively necessary to check this continued insolence."[11] A Mississippi planter who requested the aid of the governor in policing the slaves of his neighborhood did so because he thought the slaves were acting too "independently." As with the Selma editor, he understood the absence of white men in the community created greater opportunity for misbehavior, but he also blamed the presence nearby of Union troops for producing this unsettled condition.[12]

For whites the sauciness of slaves and the reluctance to submit to discipline challenged patterns of antebellum race relations, but the problem actually was part of something that was even more threatening. When they wrote of the independence of slaves, Southerners often were expressing concern with what they saw as an increasing reluctance to work by many plantation hands. Across the South, letter writers and editorialists noted that it had become more difficult to secure what was considered the proper amount of labor from their workers. Slow downs first infected the Louisiana plantations along the Mississippi River, following the passage of Admiral David Farragut's fleet upriver from New Orleans to Baton Rouge in the spring of 1862. The overseer of Magnolia Plantation left an extensive record of reports to the owners through 1862 and noted again and again his difficulties in getting the slaves to work regularly or to come out to work at all. Ultimately in October he indicated considerable frustration and complained:

*"I wish every negro would leave the place* as they will do only what pleases them, go out in the morning when it suits them, come in when they please, etc."[13]

In some circumstances, disrespect and reluctance to labor gave way to virtual rebellion. Some whites reported their slaves becoming increasingly resistant to being disciplined. A woman from Texas reported in August of 1863, after increasing Union operations along the Texas coast, that local slaves, including her own, were proving more difficult to control and refusing to submit to punishment. In several cases slaves had refused to be whipped. "Nearly all of the negros around here are at it," she wrote to her husband in the army, "some of them are getting so high in anticipation of their glorious freedom by the yankees I suppose, that they resist a whipping."[14] This resistance went so far in some cases that slaves actually threatened retaliation against those who tried to punish them. A woman in Tennessee wrote to her husband in the army in 1863 that overseers in the neighborhood were getting little labor from their slaves. She concluded that the reason was a growing reluctance to whip them. "I think it is because most every one is afraid to correct them," she wrote.[15]

Changing circumstances possibly also account for what whites considered to be an increase in slave violence against their masters. One example of this increasing resistance came from Alabama, where a woman informed her son that slaves there had threatened to kill any overseer who punished them and that others promised to burn the houses of any who whipped them.[16] In Texas a servant who had been whipped by her mistress responded by setting the house on fire at night. The mistress only with luck managed to escape.[17] These actions by slaves produced increasing fear among many whites of slave insurrections. Even though the South had seen few large-scale slave rebellions, most Southerners remained aware of the violence of the 1794 uprising led by Toussaint L'Ouverture in

*The men of the First Kansas Colored Infantry Regiment died at Poison Spring six days after hundreds of black soldiers were killed at Fort Pillow in Tennessee, a battle that has overshadowed the massacre in Arkansas. Etching from* Harper's Pictorial History of the Civil War, 1866. *(Courtesy of Don Hamilton)*

Saint-Domingue that had driven the French from the island and seen widespread violence. Through the antebellum years what happened in Saint-Domingue had been seen as the probable consequence for the South of slave insurrection and even freedom. It was a result Southerners reacted to in horror.

No massive slave insurrection took place. Instead, open hostility towards masters found other outlets when the Union Army moved into the South. Some slaves remained with their masters but provided assistance to Union forces, acting as scouts and informers. One district attorney, writing to General Winder about the disposition of a slave who had acted as a guide for Federal troops, complained of the behavior of blacks in his neighborhood. He wrote: "It is a matter of notoriety in the sections of the Confederacy where raids are frequent that the guides of the enemy are nearly always free Negroes and slaves."[18] After an early raid on the South Carolina coast, a local complained, "the people about here would not have suffered near as much if it had not been for these Negroes; in every case they have told where things have been hidden and they did most of the stealing."[19]

Thousands of slaves took further action and challenged white attitudes even more directly when they abandoned their plantations as the first opportunity arose. On the peninsula of Virginia in the spring of 1861, in western Tennessee and northern Mississippi in 1862, then along the Mississippi in 1863, thousands of slaves poured behind Union lines. There they encountered conditions that may have been worse than those faced by the slaves who remained at home. A few would even go back when they discovered that wartime freedom was not what they expected. Most did not, however. Of these, thousands actually assisted the Union war effort, working as cooks, wood cutters, teamsters, and even common laborers in support of Union armies in the field. Ultimately from these refugees the Union Army would recruit the troops that later would meet Confederate soldiers in the field.

The behavior of these "disloyal" slaves produced wide-ranging reactions among white Southerners. Southerners were not sure what it meant. Whether or not growing resistance would lead ultimately to a Southern Saint-Domingue was uncertain. Certainly it forced more Southerners to realize, as had Mary Chesnut, that they may not have known their slaves as well as they thought. Without question it disrupted the faith that many Southerners had in their slaves' loyalty and raised unsettling questions about their belief in the paternalistic compact between slave and master. Everyone was shocked at the behavior of the slaves, especially when they abandoned farm and plantation and headed for Union lines.

It is clear that their shock also was accompanied by a sense of betrayal. One woman whose husband was away in the army would write him that many in her neighborhood hoped to hide their slaves from the Yankees. She did not see how this would help, however, because she was convinced that they were not as they had seemed. Concerning her family's slaves, she informed her husband: "I don't think we have one who will stay with us," she wrote.[20] Catherine Edmondston of North Carolina would write: "[A]s to the idea of a *faithful servant, it is all a fiction*. I have seen the favorite and most petted negroes the first to leave in every instance."[21] In the Trans-Mississippi, Clara Dunlap of Ouachita County, Arkansas, believed that her slaves would remain with her as Union forces entered southwestern Arkansas in the spring of 1864. She was disappointed when they left and she found out from neighboring slaves that "*ours* intended going all the time, but kept it a secret to keep us from running them off."[22] Even an overseer in Louisiana appears to have felt betrayed by the slaves on his plantation. He reported to the owner that the field hands had engaged in widespread looting on the plantation following a Federal raid. As a result, the overseer had lost all faith in the idea that the slaves would be loyal. They were, he wrote, "the greatest hypocrites and liars that God ever made." Abandoning any pretense of paternalistic feelings, he went on to say that he now cared nothing for them "save for their work."[23]

Within the white views of race and slavery this disloyalty was understandable and predictable. The war was freeing blacks from normal discipline and, like the bad child, they increasingly would let their animal passions come to the fore. Often whites blamed the Yankees for this situation more than their slaves, but ultimately it did not matter why the discipline was being lifted. With discipline lessened, the white view predicted that the slaves would act more licentiously and violently against those around them. This presented a real threat to local communities in the eyes of many. A Mississippi planter expressed the fears born of this situation when he wrote to the governor: "[T]he question is constantly asked 'what is to become of my wife & children when left in a land swarming with negroes without a single white man on many plantations to restrain their licentiousness by a little wholesome fear.'"[24]

White ideas about slavery and race not only explained what was taking place but also provided the solution. Order would be restored when discipline was imposed. Across the South, whites responded to the disruption of slave order with efforts at imposing harsher controls on slaves. Most Confederate state governments responded to growing concerns by imposing more restrictions on slaves, particularly on their movement in the countryside. The instrument of enforcement on such measures was the slave patrol, and everywhere governments increased patrol efforts. Typically, before the war most states required that precinct patrols ride once a month to look for stray slaves or slaves who might be up to no good. Wartime patrols were increased to once a week. Prior to the war, many citizens appear to have shirked their duties to ride patrol. Now state legislatures increased penalties on those who failed to serve. Some states even assigned policing slaves as an additional duty of the local militia. In Arkansas, the wartime legislature tried to ensure that control began at the lowest level when it passed an act requiring every plantation to have present on it at least one white person who was capable of preserving order among the slaves. All of this indicated the awareness that control was being threatened and that it had to be maintained. The one action of the Confederacy that most reflected these concerns was the exclusion from conscription of

*The backbone of the Southern cotton industry was African slave labor, as shown in this antebellum etching. (Courtesy of the Arkansas History Commission)*

one white man for every twenty slaves on a farm or plantation. Ironically, this action actually produced conflict among whites when it raised issues of class among many of the South's non-slaveholders.[25]

Ultimately, most whites realized that increasing police measures would not restore discipline or a return to the way things had been. The combination of the sense of betrayal generated by slave behavior that many whites felt and the perception of the existence of a violent threat posed by free slaves led to significant changes in the basic relationship between masters and the entire Southern white community and the slaves. Within the Southern frame of reference, slaves who had proven faithless had surrendered the right to the master's protection. Freed of a sense of obligation, many masters appear to have changed during the war. Slaves believed that whites blamed them for what was happening and turned their frustrations on them. Many masters appeared quick to express their anger and frustration with violence. A Texas slave recalled that as the war progressed and the master left for the army, the mistress increasingly blamed her slaves for the war and her problems. The result was that the mistress was "meaner'n the devil all the time. Seems like she jus' hated us worser than ever."[26] Another slave believed that his master changed after his two sons enlisted in the army. "Marster Charley cuss everything and every body and us watch out and keep out of his way." On learning of the death of one of the sons, the same slave reported that his master became even more violent. He struck one of his female slaves crying out, "`Free de nigger, will dey? I free dem.'...Him takes de gun offen de rack and starts for de field whar de niggers am a'working.'"[27] Another slave reported a mistress whose anger also boiled over upon learning of the death of her son. This mistress whipped her slaves "till she shore nuff wore out."[28] Another South Carolina slave reported that as Union forces moved into the neighborhood his owner called his slaves into the yard and "showed them a big sack of money, what they had made for him, and told him dat he was gwin to kill all of them befo' de Yankees set them free and that they woudn't need no money after they was done dead." The slave was convinced that only the master's death two days later prevented him carrying out his threat.[29]

For the individual slave who provoked a master, the results could be violent and often times deadly. Slaves reported numerous incidents in which slaves, emboldened by the changing circumstances of the war, stood up to their masters only to be killed. A Louisiana slave remembered that when the slaves on his plantation heard about the war and came to understand that it would free them, they would go into the woods and pray for freedom to "come quick." They were careful to make sure that the master did not know of these meetings "for if massa find out he whip all of us, sho'."[30] A North Carolina slave remembered that the hands on his plantation "knew what all the fightin' was about, but they didn't dare say anything. The man who owned the slaves was too mad as it was, and if the niggers say anything they get shot right then and thar."[31] On a Virginia plantation, a master's two sons beat a slave who they had heard had prayed for the Yankees. When they demanded that he pray for the Confederacy, the slave refused. The two then took turns whipping him until he collapsed and died.[32] A North Carolina slave recalled when one of the master's sons who had joined the army came back in uniform, one of the slaves muttered "Look at dat God damn sojer. He fightin' to keep us niggahs from bein' free." The young soldier responded with outrage and despite his mother's efforts at intervening "picked up de gun an' shot er hole in Leonard's ches' big as yo' fis'."[33]

As violence on the plantation increased in an effort to maintain order or as an expression of growing frustration and hostility towards the slaves, the surrounding community responded in like manner. Slave disobedience and disloyalty in the midst of war presented a challenge not just to the authority of the master but the well-being of the community. A dialogue between the well-known Georgia minister Charles Colcock Jones and his son reflected the growing concern and the developing view that the community had to act in cases where slaves showed greater independence and especially in dealing with runaways. In the past, a runaway would simply be captured and returned to a master. To put to death a slave was to deprive a master of his property. The elder Jones now wondered if running away should not be treated as insurrection, describing runaways as "traitors who may pilot an enemy into your *bed chamber*! They know every road and swamp and creek and plantation in the county, and are the worst of spies."[34] He asked further if "they declare themselves enemies and at war with owners by going over to the enemy who is seeking both our lives and property."[35] Reverend Jones asked his lawyer son whether or not such men could not be dealt with summarily by citizens, and the younger Jones, after injecting some legal warnings, concluded that in the absence of courts citizens must act and decisively. "If insensible to every other consideration," he wrote, "terror must be made to operate upon their minds, and fear prevent what curiosity and desire for utopian pleasures induce them to attempt."[36] Jones's son warned that the "ignorance, credulity, pliability, desire for change, the absence of the political ties of allegiance, the peculiar status of the race" should be considered in administering punishment, but if it was clear the slave knew what he or she was doing, the slave should "undoubtedly suffer death."[37]

Most Southern communities did not debate their responsibility but acted. In Georgetown, South Carolina, three slaves who had escaped came back to take their wives to freedom and were caught by the local provost martial. The local provost martial court heard testimony on their actions and then sentenced them to death, carrying out the sentence quickly to avoid any pleas for executive clemency by the men's owner.[38] A similar incident took place in Lawrence County, Mississippi, when a returning slave was seized by local whites and lynched.[39] In September 1864, when thirty slaves stole their master's guns and rode towards the Mississippi River from Amite County, Mississippi, Confederate troops were sent in pursuit. When they found the fleeing men, a fight took place in which all but a few who escaped to the river were killed.[40] In Bladen County, North Carolina, whites rounded up hundreds of slaves who were supposed to be involved in a conspiracy to rise up against whites at Christmas time and massacre them. At least six were hanged and a local citizen informed the governor that it was "more than probable the whole of them will be hung by the enraged populace without the form or sanction of the Civil Law."[41] A plot in Brooks County, Georgia, met with similar violence. A crowd arrested the accused and immediately hanged three of those seized.[42] In South Carolina, local Confederate forces pretending to be Yankees tricked a slave into revealing his sympathies by calling on him to help locate a Confederate camp. His arrival proved his treachery and the scouts immediately lynched him.[43]

Given the view white Southerners held of slaves who ran away and their response, it is not surprising that they would see an even greater threat in late 1862 and 1863 when they learned of the Emancipation Proclamation and Union Army efforts to raise troops among the South's slaves. In August 1862, Secretary of War Henry Stanton authorized the recruitment on the South Carolina coastal islands of five thousand freedmen as soldiers. Subsequently, Nathaniel Banks created his "Corps d'Afrique" in Louisiana, George Stearns of Massachusetts began recruiting black soldiers in Nashville, and commanders in Virginia and coastal North Carolina also formed black regiments. The most significant effort, however, was made by General Lorenzo Thomas in the Mississippi Valley, who raised

**Jefferson county, June 9, 1851.        6—5w.**

# Runaway Negro In Jail.

WAS committed to the Jail of Saline county, as a runaway, on the 8th day of June, 1851, a negro man, who says his name is JOHN, and that he belongs to *Henry Johnson*, of Desha county, Ark. He is aged about 24 or 25 years, straight in stature, quick spoken, looks very fierce out of his eyes, and plays on the fiddle. Had on, when apprehended, white cotton pants, coarse cotton shirt, and black hat. The owner is hereby notified to come forward, prove property, and pay the expenses of committal and advertisement, otherwise the said negro will be dealt with according to law. THOMAS PACK, *Sheriff and Jailor of Saline county.*

**Benton, June 21, 1851.        7—26w.**

*Advertisements noting the escape or capture of runaway slaves were common in antebellum Arkansas newspapers. Many of the soldiers serving in the First Kansas Colored Infantry were escaped slaves from Arkansas and Missouri. (Courtesy of the Butler Center for Arkansas Studies, Central Arkansas Library System, Little Rock)*

over seventy-six thousand black troops beginning in the spring of 1863. Ultimately, black troops would constitute about ten percent of the total force in the Union Army. Many of these soldiers served with distinction, beginning with the accolades they received at Port Hudson on May 27, 1863. Their service there convinced many doubters in the Union Army that these troops would fight. Ultimately about two hundred thousand African-Americans served in the Union Army and provided a significant contribution to the ultimate war effort.[44]

Within the framework of attitudes created before the war and developing during it, the Union Army's decision to enroll black troops produced inevitable reactions among Southern whites. The use of African-American soldiers was not simply the utilization of another source of manpower; for white Southerners it represented the raising of the South's slave population in servile insurrection, the ultimate threat to society. In the white Southerner's mind, this meant that the true animal nature of blacks would be unleashed and result in a reign of violence and debauchery. One Georgia soldier heard of the Emancipation Proclamation while with Lee's Army at Fredericksburg in February 1863. His reaction was a reaffirmation of his intention to fight to the death. He wrote to his wife: "[W]here is the man that desurves[sic] the name of a man that would not fight a nation who would try to raise [slave] insurrection among women and children."[45]

In the end, the idea of confronting black soldiers produced anger and outrage among most Confederate soldiers. A Kentuckian shared his feelings with his diary in June of 1864 after encountering black troops: "Great Jehoshaphat!" he wrote. "My blood boils to think of it!!"[46] Most also expressed a belief that an encounter with blacks would produce extreme violence and that the rules of civilized warfare might not apply. A Mississippi soldier had not yet encountered black troops but he shared the intensity of his feelings when he wrote to his mother about the prospect: "I hope I may never see a Negro Soldier or I cannot be...a Christian Soldier."[47] One soldier who saw black soldiers as dupes of the Yankees nonetheless wrote: "[I]f the U.S. should, as it seams [sic] they are determined to[,] send negroes to fight the South. Just as sure as they ever do, I intend to make wool fly if I ever get a chance."[48]

The grave character of the perceived threat helps to explain why the Confederacy's first official response to the enrollment of black troops was to take measures that might dissuade the

North from acting. President Jefferson Davis first ordered that black troops would be dealt with as insurrectionaries. This would have meant that they would have been turned over to state authorities for punishment. Davis also ordered that white Union officers who led such troops would be turned over to the same state authorities and prosecuted under state laws dealing with anyone who incited slaves to insurrection. The punishment in such cases was death. Confederate Secretary of War James Seddon had to deal with the first captured black soldier in the autumn of 1862, proposing that he be "executed as an example" to other slaves. It appears that as many as five blacks were executed under these policies. Only Abraham Lincoln's threat to meet execution with execution led to a reversal.[49]

Nonetheless, given changing white attitudes about slaves, the feelings among Confederate soldiers about black troops, and considering the initial public policy announced by the Confederate government, it should not be surprising that in any confrontation between Confederate soldiers and U.S. Colored Troops there was a possibility for fighting to move beyond the bounds of civilized warfare. The evidence is overwhelming that barbaric incidents took place in many of these engagements, the one at Poison Spring, Arkansas, included.

On the other hand, often combat between black and white soldiers never rose to this level of violence. Ultimately, the question that historians must examine more closely is not whether or not massacres happened but what conditions made them happen. It must be remembered such behavior clearly was outside even the rules of warfare accepted by the Confederacy, especially after the reversal of policy at Richmond in 1862. In effect, within the definitions of the Confederate Army, these were war crimes. Officers should have stepped in to keep them from happening or at least to stop them. Yet massacres happened anyway. Did they take place when the fury generated by battle melded with that created by racial hostility to produce battles that ran out of the control of officers? Or were they the result of more self-conscious and cold-blooded efforts at punishing blacks who had risen up against their masters? This would seem to be a more fruitful line of inquiry.

A preliminary assessment of the evidence gives no simple answer to these questions and even raises other issues. Evidence exists that shows different things happened in different battles. In some instances, it appears that black troops were shot down or bayoneted because officers lost control of a battle and could not bring their men back under control. The fight at the Crater on July 30, 1864, best illustrates this situation, although it also is the one battle for which the most primary sources exist to examine circumstances. That battle involved the Army of Northern Virginia's first face-to-face encounter with black troops. Following the explosion of the mine under Confederate lines around Petersburg, Federal troops were sent to take the area and included among the troops was a division of United States Colored Troops. Confederate participants in the battle attested to the outrage felt among the troops when they encountered these former slaves. One Georgia sergeant would write that "Negro troops were in the fray, they threw away their guns and attempted to surrender, but our men replied that they had arms and must fight, and continued to shoot them down."[50]

The Crater was the work of soldiers in battle, however, and their officers tried to stop what was happening. In this case they ultimately succeeded. According to John Brooks of Cobb's Legion Cavalry, Confederate forces "were persisting in the final destruction of the...undeserving captives, when Gen. William Mahone with drawn sabre and awful threats caused them to desist from their barbarous work."[51] W.C. McClellan would write of it more directly when he told his father that all of the black prisoners "would have been killed had it not been for gen Mahone who beg our men to Spare them." Mahone told one of McClellan's comrades "for God's sake stop." The man replied,

"Well gen let me kill one more [and] he deliberately took out his pocket knife and cut one's Throat."[52]

A similar example of how racial views intensified the character of battle and led to greater carnage occurred in the confrontation between whites and blacks at the Battle of Nashville on December 15, 1864. A soldier who had served with the Thirteenth Arkansas and then the Washington Artillery later recalled the "Negro charge." "This was the first time that we of the Army of Tennessee had ever met our former slaves in battle," he wrote. "It excited in our men the intensest indignation, but that indignation expressed itself in a way peculiarly ominous and yet quite natural for the 'masters.' As soon as it was found out that the men advancing upon them were Negroes, a deliberate policy was adopted. It was to let them come almost to the works before a shot was to be fired, and then the whole line was to rise up and empty their guns into them…crash went that deadly volley of lead full into the poor fellows' faces. The carnage was awful."[53] Another soldier reported that when the Confederates counterattacked, the men advanced, yelling, "no quarter—to niggers."[54]

Evidence concerning the best-known massacre of black troops, that at Fort Pillow on April 12, 1864, is less clear. A Congressional investigation concluded that Confederate soldiers not only shot down black soldiers who surrendered in battle but continued their slaughter long afterwards. The report charged that some wounded soldiers had been burned to death when Confederates set fire to their barracks and that other wounded soldiers had been buried alive. There is no question that surrendering black soldiers were murdered. Statistics indicated that while nearly sixty percent of the white soldiers in the garrison were taken as prisoners, only twenty percent of blacks were captured. A Confederate soldier who had participated described what happened: "[T]he poor, deluded negroes would run up to our men, fall upon their knees and with uplifted hands scream for mercy, but were ordered to their feet and shot down."[55] On the other hand, most of the other charges proved more difficult to prove.[56]

There are less ambiguous cases. In some battles, the killing continued long after the heat of battle had cooled down and in such cases it is hard to argue that anything took place but cold-blooded murder. In a skirmish between black troops and Confederates in East Florida on February 20, 1864, some of the former were captured. A Georgia soldier informed his wife: "Our men killed some of them after they had fell in our hands wounded."[57] The evidence further suggests that in some cases officers not only failed to suppress the violence but may actually have ordered it. Following the battle of Saltville in Virginia on October 2, 1864, a Kentucky officer wrote in his diary that General Felix H. Robertson rode up to him and told him that in the battle between his troops and black soldiers "he had killed nearly all the negroes."[58] The Kentuckian indicated that on the next day "Scouts were sent, & went all over the field, and the continued ring of the rifle, sung the death knell of many a poor negro who was unfortunate enough not to be killed yesterday. Our men took no negro prisoners. Great numbers of them were killed yesterday & today."[59]

Such actions may be difficult to understand from the modern perspective. Within a historical framework, however, such violence is much easier to grasp. Given what whites of the time believed about blacks and their understanding of the implications of black behavior at the time, black-white confrontations always contained within them the potential for barbarism. Rather than debate whether or not such events took place, scholars might more fruitfully accept the reality of such events and move on to an assessment of what produced particular instances of barbarity. What kept some confrontations from breaking down into massacres? What limited the violence in other cases? What extended it in others? Framed in such a

way, history might better help us understand the role of race in
Civil War battles.

≈

1. Leon Litwack, *Been in the Storm So Long: The Aftermath of Slavery* (New York: Alfred A. Knopf, 1979), 4.

2. Speech in Michael Perman, ed., *Major Problems in the Civil War and Reconstruction* (Lexington, Mass.: D.C. Heath and Company, 1991), 280.

3. Quoted in James L. Roark, *Masters Without Slaves: Southern Planters in the Civil War and Reconstruction* (New York: W.W. Norton & Company, 1977), 102.

4. For an assessment of the idea of paternalism see Eugene Genovese, *The World the Slaveholders Made: Two Essays in Interpretation* (New York, 1969). For other examinations of white attitudes towards African-Americans, see George M. Frederickson, *The Black Image in the White Mind: The Debate on Afro-American Character and Destiny, 1817-1914* (New York: Oxford University Press, 1971) and William S. Jenkins, *Pro-Slavery Thought in the Old South* (Chapel Hill: University of North Carolina Press, 1935).

5. Litwack, 7.

6. Quoted in Bell I. Wiley, *Southern Negroes, 1861-1865* (New Haven: Yale University Press, 1933), 70.

7. Quoted in Litwack, 16.

8. Ibid., 16.

9. C. Vann Woodward, ed., *Mary Chesnut's Civil War* (New Haven: Yale University Press, 1981), 48.

10. Diary of Betty Herndon Maury, April 25, 1862, Library of Congress.

11. Selma (Alabama) *Morning Reporter*, August 27, 1863, quoted in Wiley, 72.

12. Isaac Applewhite to Governor Pettus, June 6, 1862, Governors' Papers, series E, no. 57, Mississippi State Archives.

13. Magnolia Plantation Records, October 18, 1862, quoted in Wiley, 74.

14. Lizzie to Dear Will, August 13, 1863 (Grimes County), in Erika L. Murr, ed., *A Rebel Wife in Texas: The Diary and Letters of Elizabeth Scott Neblett, 1852-1864* (Baton Rouge: Louisiana State University Press, 2001), 134-5.

15. Mrs. James Abernethy to her husband, January 11, 1863, Abernethy Papers, quoted in Wiley, 76.

16. Mrs. C.C. Clay, Sr., to C.C. Clay, Jr., September 5, 1863, Clement Claiborne Clay Papers, Perkins Library, Duke University.

17. Murr, 306.

18. U.S. War Department, *The War of the Rebellion: A Compilation of the Official Records of the Union and Confederate Armies* series 2, vol. VI, (Washington, D.C.: U.S. Government Printing Office, 1880-1901), 1053 (hereafter referred to as *Official Records*).

19. Charlotte Ravenell, *Two Diaries from Middle St. John's, Berkeley, South Carolina, Feb-May, 1865: Journals Kept by Susan R. Jervey and Miss Charlotte St. J. Raveneli* (Pinoplis, S.C.: St. John's Hunting Club, 1921), 35.

20. Lizzie to Dear Will, August 13, 1866, Murr, 135.

21. Catherine Ann Edmonston Diaries, February 12, 1862; March 31, 1862; May 10. 1862; September 9, 1862; in Beth G. Crabtree and James W. Patton, eds., *Journal of a Secesh Lady: The Diary of Catherine Ann Devereux Edmondston, 1860-1866* (Raleigh: Division of Archives and History, 1979).

22. Clara Dunlap to My dear Sister, July 24, 1864, in Sarah M. Fountain, ed., *Sisters, Seeds, & Cedars: Rediscovering Nineteenth-Century Life Through Correspondence from Rural Arkansas and Alabama* (Conway: University of Central Arkansas Press, 1995), 156.

23. G.P. Whitting, ed., "Letters from John H. Ransdell to Gov. Thomas O. Moore, dated 1863," *Louisiana Historical Quarterly* XIV (Oct. 1931), 491-502.

24. Brigadier General Richard Winter to Governor John J. Pettus, June 6, 1862, in John K. Bettersworth and James K. Silver, eds., *Mississippi in the Confederacy* (Jackson: Mississippi Department of Archives and History, 1961), 77.

25. See Wiley, 34-35; *Acts of Arkansas, 1861*, Spec. Sess., no. 41, sec. 1.

26. John Rawick, ed., *American Slave: Texas Narrative* V, part 4, (first quote) 192, 193-4.

27. Ibid. V, part 3 (second quote), 260.

28. Litwack, 10.

29. Rawick, *American Slave* vol. 3, part 4, 27 (hereafter referred to as *American Slave*).

30. *American Slave* V, part 4. 154.

31. *American Slave* XIV, part 1, 144.

32. Quoted in Litwack, 30.

33. Reminiscence of Fanny Cannady in W. Buck Yearns and John G. Barrett, *North Carolina Civil War Documentary* (Chapel Hill: University of North Carolina Press, 1980), 259-60.

34. C.C. Jones to C.C. Jones, Jr., July 10, 1862, in Robert M. Meyers, ed., *Children of Pride: Letters of the Family of the Rev. Dr. Charles Colcock Jones from the Years 1860-1868, Abridged Edition* (New Haven: Yale University Press, 1984), 277.

35. C.C. Jones to C.C. Jones, Jr., July 21, 1862, ibid., 282.

36. C.C. Jones, Jr. to C.C. Jones, July 25, 1862, ibid., 286.

37. C.C. Jones, Jr. to C.C. Jones, July 19, 1862, ibid., 281-2.

38. Litwack, 55.

39. *American Slave*, supp. 1, VI, part 1, 182.

40. H. Clessedy to Governor Clark, September 12, 1864, Governor's Papers, series E, no. 66, Mississippi State Archives.

41. Henry Nutt to Z.B. Vance, December 12, 1864, quoted in Yearns and Barrett, 257.

42. *Southern Recorder*, August 30, 1864.

43. Ravenall, 18 (diary of Miss Susan R. Jervey) in Wiley, 68.

44. Estimates on the number of black soldiers who served in the Union armed forces vary. James M. McPherson wrote in *Ordeal By Fire: The Civil War and Reconstruction* (New York: McGraw-Hill, Inc., 1992, 353) that 179,000 soldiers and 10,000 sailors fought for the Union. More recently, Russell F. Weigley contends in *A Great Civil War: A Military and Political History, 1861-1865* (Bloomington: Indiana University Press, 2000, 190) that 186,017 blacks served in the army and an indeterminate but large additional number were less formally organized.

45. W.R. Stillwell to My Dear Mollie, February 10, 1863, W[illiam] R[oss] Stillwell Letters, typescript in Georgia Department of Archives and History, Atlanta (hereafter cited as GDAH).

46. William C. Davis and Meredith L. Swentor, eds., *Bluegrass Confederate: The Headquarters Diary of Edward O. Guerrant* (Baton Rouge: Louisiana State University Press, 1999), 486.

47. Jerome Yates to his mother, August 10, 1864, Confederate States of America Collection, Center for American Studies, University of Texas at Austin.

48. W.R. Stillwell to My Dear Mollie, February 10, 1863, in W[illiam] R[oss] Stillwell Letters, GDAH.

49. Russell F. Weigley, *The Great Civil War: A Military and Political History, 1861-1865* (Bloomington and Indianapolis: Indiana University Press, 2000), 189.

50. A.B. Simms to his sister, August 1, 1864, in June Peacock, "A Georgian's View of War," 115, quoted in J. Tracy Power, *Lee's Miserables: Life in the Army of Northern Virginia from the Wilderness to Appomattox* (Chapel Hill: University of North Carolina Press, 1998), 139.

51. N.J. Brooks Diary, July 30, 1864, Brooks Papers, Southern Historical Collection, University of North Carolina at Chapel Hill.

52. W.C. McClellan to Robert McClellan, August 15, 1864, privately held manuscript quoted in Wiley, *The Life of Johnny Reb* (New York: Doubleday & Company, Inc.), 315.

53. Nathaniel Cheairs Hughes, Jr., ed., *The Civil War Memoir of Philip Daingerfield Stephenson, D.D.* (Conway: University of Central Arkansas Press, 1995), 320.

54. Clyde C. Walton, *Private Smith's Journal: Recollections of the Late War* (Chicago: R.R. Donnelley, 1963), 195-96, quoted in Reid Mitchell, *Civil War Soldiers: Their Expectations and Their Experiences* (New York: Viking, 1988), 175.

55. Quote from Shelby Foote, *The Civil War, A Narrative: Red River to Appomattox* (New York: Vintage, 1974), 112.

56. For a discussion of the most recent scholarship on Fort Pillow, see John Cimprich and Robert C. Mainfort, Jr., "Fort Pillow Revisited: New Evidence about an Old Controversy," *Civil War History* 28 (Dec., 1982), 293-306; Albert Castel, "The Fort Pillow Massacre: A Fresh Examination of the Evidence," ibid., 4 (March 1958), 37-50.

57. J.M. Jordan to My Dear Louisia, February 21, 1864, in James M. (Matt) Jordan Letters, GDAH.

58. Davis and Swentor, 545.

59. Ibid., 546.

# The Changing Role of Blacks in the Civil War

## Ronnie A. Nichols

LET THE SLAVE AND FREE COLORED PEOPLE BE CALLED INTO SERVICE, AND FORMED INTO A LIBERATION ARMY, To march into the South and raise the banner of emancipation among the slaves.

—Frederick Douglass
*Douglass' Monthly*, May 1861[1]

During America's Revolutionary War and the War of 1812, men of African descent served faithfully and gallantly, with some making the ultimate sacrifice for freedom.[2] However, African service in the U.S. Army ended on February 20, 1820, when an order handed down by the U.S. War Department stated "…that no Negro or mulatto would be received as a recruit of the Army." In a word, the act told the five thousand Negroes who saw service in the War of Independence—all of whom were freed after the war—not only that their services were no longer needed, but that they were not worthy to serve in the militia of the United States.[3] These veterans lived "free" in America as quasi-citizens, with the majority of black Americans remaining in slavery.

Negro men could not and did not serve in the war with Mexico, which ended in 1848. As a result of the Mexican War, the United States grew in size, number of states, and population; the number of slaves and free Negroes increased as well. During this period of expansion, the elusive "slave question"

*Before they were recruited as soldiers, black "contrabands of war" were utilized as labor-
ers by the Federal army. Southern forces also used black labor in their war efforts. This
image from a German-language edition of* Frank Leslie's Illustrated Newspaper
*shows a work crew at Fort Monroe in Virginia. (Courtesy of Frank Latimer)*

taxed Congress and the nation. The Missouri Compromise,
enacted in 1820, was to prohibit slavery to the north of
Missouri's southern boundary, but many slave owners did not
find these boundaries acceptable. The Compromise of 1850, a
national Fugitive Slave Law, threatened the lives and liberties of
almost all free blacks. Legislation forming the Compromise of
1850 admitted California as a free state and organized the New
Mexico and Utah territories without restriction on slavery. But
the compromise also included a harsh new fugitive slave law
that allowed Southerners to recapture runaway slaves even in
free states and made it a crime for anyone to aid a runaway.
Some of the black people dragged back into slavery under the
new law had been living free for years.[4]

The U.S. Supreme Court decision of March 6, 1857, in the Dred Scott case in essence rendered anyone of African descent a non-citizen, "...that unfortunate race...they had had no rights which the white man was bound to respect."[5] This "unfortunate race" had now become a people in a land without a country.

Arkansas, in response to the Dred Scott decision, passed legislation to expel all free Negroes by January 1860; those who remained had to submit to the institution of slavery. One hundred and forty-four people of African descent had been identified as free. These free Negroes paid taxes and some owned property. However, they could not vote, bear arms, nor benefit from protection under the law, enduring taxation without representation. The displaced freemen found little solace elsewhere:

> FREE BLACKS OUSTED FROM ARKANSAS TURN WEST
> From this terrible injustice we appeal to the moral sentiment of the world. We turn to the free North; but even here oppression tracks our steps. Indiana shuts her door upon us. Illinois denies us admission to her prairie homes. Oregon refuses us an abiding place for the soles of our weary feet. And even Minnesota has our exclusion under consideration...
> *The Principia*, February 11, 1860

The Rebel attack on Fort Sumter, South Carolina, on April 12, 1861, and Lincoln's call for seventy-five thousand militia to put down the rebellion plunged America into Civil War. This call from the president also fell upon the ears and hearts of the sons and grandsons of those soldiers of African descent who had participated in this country's early conflicts. By law, it had been more than forty years since they had been allowed to serve in the Army. What role would people of African descent play in this Civil War?

# An Arkansas Proposal

Ironically, the first proposal to raise black troops was made for the Confederate States of America. On July 17, 1861, W.S. Turner of Helena, Arkansas, submitted the following letter:

Hon. L. P. Walker:

DEAR SIR: I wrote you a few days since for myself and many others in this district to ascertain if we could get Negro regiments received for Confederate service, officered, of course, by white men. All we ask is arms, clothing, and provisions, and usual pay for officers and not one cent pay for Negroes. Our Negroes are too good to fight Lincoln hirelings, but as they pretend to love Negroes so much we want to show them how much the true Southern cotton-patch Negro loves them in return....And now, sir, if you can receive the Negroes that can be raised we will soon give the Northern thieves a gorge of the Negroes' love for them that will never be forgotten. As you well know, I have had long experience with Negro character. I am satisfied; they are easy disciplined and less trouble than whites in camp, and will fight desperately as long as they have a single white officer living. I know one man that will furnish and arm 100 of his own and his son for their captain. The sooner we bring a strong Negro force against the hirelings the sooner we shall have peace, in my humble judgment. Let me hear from you.

Your old friend,

W.S. Turner[6]

Turner's proposal was quickly rejected:

Confederate States of America
War Department
Richmond, August 2, 1861
W.S. TURNER, Helena, Ark.:

SIR: In reply to your letter of the 17th of July I am directed by the Secretary of War to say that this Department is not prepared to accept the Negro regiment tendered by you, and yet it is not doubted that almost every slave would cheerfully aid his master in the work of hurling back the fanatical invader. Moreover, if the necessity were apparent there is high authority for the employment of such forces.

Washington himself recommended the enlistment of two Negro regiments in Georgia, and the Congress sanctioned the measure. But now there is a superabundance of our own color tendering their services to the Government in its day of peril and ruthless invasion, a superabundance of men when we are bound to admit the inadequate supply of arms at present at the disposal of the Government.[7]

Respectfully,

A.T. BLEDSOE

Chief of Bureau of War

In the city of New Orleans in May 1861, free men of African, French, and Spanish blood organized themselves into the Native Guards, a Louisiana militia. When they offered their services to the Confederacy, they received less than a lukewarm reception. However, these men who had armed themselves with personal arms and purchased their own uniforms would be found by Union forces in April of 1862 serving under the Confederate flag.[8]

This conflict apparently was not just a war where "brothers fought against brothers"—it was "a white man's war." President Lincoln had made it clear that the war was not being fought to end slavery. He had to consider the border states of Kentucky, Missouri, Delaware, and Maryland, which remained in the Union while maintaining the institution of slavery. Lincoln ordered a draft of three hundred thousand militia on August 4, 1862 (which never went into effect). On the same day, the president told a delegation of "Western gentlemen" that he was not prepared to enlist Negroes as soldiers, refusing their offer of two Negro regiments.

However, some Americans of African descent did manage to join the newly forming volunteer regiments. In President Lincoln's home state, H. Ford Douglas, a runaway slave and abolitionist orator, enlisted in a white unit, Company G of the Ninety-fifth Illinois Volunteer Infantry. Douglas viewed the Civil War thus: "[I] play my part in the great drama of the

Negro's redemption." He also saw the war as schoolmaster to
Abraham Lincoln, which would "... educate the President out
of his 'pro-slavery' ideas about employing Negroes as soldiers."[9]

## A Force to be Reckoned With

From the first salvo of the Civil War, both North and South
had to consider the economic and military potential of the
4,441,830 souls of African origin who lived in the United
States. Their numbers made up over fourteen percent of the
nation's population of 31,443,321. The eleven states compris-
ing the Confederacy contained 3,521,110 Negro slaves and
132,760 free Negroes. In other words, more than ninety
percent of America's black population was in the South and in
bondage.[10]

Arkansas, one of the last southern states to join the
Confederacy, recorded a population of 435,258; of this number
111,115 were slaves and 144 were free Negroes. These
Arkansas slaves were valued at $77,780,500, or on average
$700 each.[11] In 1860, Arkansas slaves produced 367,393 bales
of ginned cotton with a market value of $16,165,292.[12]

The Civil War was viewed by enslaved people of African
descent as the opportunity to gain freedom and by free blacks
as a chance to strike a blow for the freedom of others of their
race. The invading Union armies were seen as a haven for
runaway slaves. Union General Benjamin F. Butler set a prece-
dent on May 24, 1861, when he refused to return three
runaway slaves to their master, a Confederate colonel. Butler's
reason for not complying was that these runaways were of
service to a military officer of a "foreign" government.
Therefore, they were instruments of war to be taken or confiscated once they came under Union control. General Butler
labeled these runaway slaves as "contrabands"—a term that

would spread quickly to all who were identified or claimed to have been put to work for the Confederacy. Butler's policy became law on August 6, 1861, when the United States Congress passed the first Confiscation Act. The act specifically included slaves who had been "employed in or on forts...or any military or naval service of the Confederacy."[13] The Confiscation Act did not explicitly declare such slaves free, but it nullified all claims by the masters to their labor. However, the Union army had to enforce all federal laws (including fugitive slave laws) in the slave border states that remained in the Union. Prior to the Confiscation Act, the 3,521,110 slaves behind the Confederate lines worked as laborers, food producers, and plantation and factory foremen. These black laborers freed the maximum number of white Southerners to carry arms.

By 1862, the first Confiscation Act had an eroding effect on the Confederacy as it began to strip the South of its black labor force. As Union troops moved into more southern territories, the contrabands flocked to the invading Yankees. The war had also devoured men and supplies, of both North and South, beyond expectations. Now the ebb and flow of America's black population had an impact. While Southern planters tried to move their slaves to keep them from being confiscated, a great number of slaves removed themselves by running away. This black migration within the geographical area of the South was an economic and psychological blow to the Confederacy. At the same time, the Union generals were being challenged with fighting a war, occupying new territory, and having to care for contrabands.

The second Confiscation Act, approved on July 17, 1862, declared slaves owned by disloyal masters "forever free of their servitude" and ordered that they be "not again held as slaves." The act also authorized the president to employ "persons of African descent" in any capacity to suppress the rebellion. Also on this date, the Militia Act became law, providing for the employment of blacks in any military or naval service "for which they may be competent" and granting freedom to slave men so employed, as well as to families if they too were owned by disloyal masters.[14] The new act effectively ended more than forty years of exclusion from the armed forces for men of African descent.

In the Trans-Mississippi West, some of the first blacks to serve in the U.S. Army were runaway slaves from Arkansas, Missouri, and Indian Territory who had made their way to Kansas. In August 1862, some of these men became the initial members of the First Kansas Colored Volunteer Infantry, even though there was no official policy for enlisting black men in the U.S. Army. Lincoln had appointed Senator James H. Lane as the recruiting commissioner in Kansas; after his appointment, Lane recruited black men as part of his cavalry unit, and organized the First Kansas over the objection of the president. Lane answered those who opposed his policy and actions by saying that a Negro could "just as well become food for powder...as my son." In addition to Lane, two other Union generals organized black regiments in 1862 without official approval from Washington. David Hunter began organizing the First South Carolina Volunteers—the first black regiment— on May 9, and Benjamin Butler issued a call to the free blacks of New Orleans on August 22. (Many of these men had originally offered their military services to the Confederacy.)[15]

In Arkansas, Major General Samuel Ryan Curtis and the Army of the Southwest witnessed thousands of slaves being drawn to them. One Midwestern soldier wrote: "The slaves seem to understand the matter very clearly and are on the alert to make escape by any opportunity." General Curtis, a former congressman from Iowa and a staunch abolitionist, also supported the use of soldiers of African descent. On July 31, 1862, he wrote from Helena to Major General Henry W. Halleck in Washington, D.C.:

GENERAL: ...I have given free papers to negroes who were mustered by the rebel masters to blockade my way to my supplies. These negroes prisoners were the most efficient foes I had to encounter; they are now throwing down their axes and rushing in for free papers.[16]

The August 22, 1862, *Memphis Daily Appeal* published a purported emancipation order and pass from Curtis:

SPECIAL ORDER NO. 157

Jerry White, a colored man, formerly a slave, having by direction of owner (has) been engaged in rebel service, is permitted to pass the pickets of the command northward, and is forever emancipated from his master, who permitted him to assist in attempting to break up the government and laws of the country. By command of

MAJOR–GENERAL CURTIS

And, while General Curtis was carrying out his own illegal emancipation of former slaves through "free papers," General Lane's unauthorized black regiment advanced into Missouri.

## *African–American Soldiers in Combat*

The First Kansas Colored Volunteer Infantry Regiment engaged Confederate guerrillas in Clay County, Missouri, on October 7 and on the Osage River in Bates County, Missouri, on October 27, 1862, "the first time in the war that Northern Negroes saw action as soldiers."

The reality of black soldiers fighting for the Union army in Arkansas was noted at the Battle of Prairie Grove, Arkansas, on December 7, 1862. The (U.S.) First Indian Home Guards had a number of black Indians or native people of African blood in their ranks, a revelation that received attention in the following notice in the December 27, 1862, *Arkansas State Gazette*:

NEGRO SOLDIERS IN THE ABOLITION RANKS.—
*The following is an extract of a letter from Confederate officer, who participated in the bloody battle at Prairie Grove, on the 7th inst.:*
"I saw two dead Negroes, dressed in federal uniforms with swords on— officers, most likely. The idea of free–born Americans fighting such, is disgusting."

On New Year's Day 1863, the idea of freedom moved closer to reality when President Lincoln fulfilled his pledge to free slaves in the rebellious states with the Emancipation Proclamation. The proclamation not only freed slaves in states in rebellion, it also allowed that "such persons, of suitable condition, will be received into the armed services of the United States, to garrison forts, positions, stations, and other places, and to man vessels of all sorts in said services." At Fort Scott, Kansas, on January 1, 1863, Captain William D. Matthews, Company D, First Kansas Colored, after the reading of the Emancipation Proclamation, wrote: "Today is a day for great rejoicing with us. As a thinking man I never

*William D. Matthews recruited dozens of men for service with the First Kansas Colored Volunteer Infantry. (Courtesy of the Kansas State Historical Society, Topeka, Kansas)*

doubted this day would come...Now is our time to strike. Our own exertions and our own muscle must make us men. If we fight we shall be respected. I see that a well–licked man respects the one who thrashes him." (Matthews, a black man from Maryland, raised sixty-seven men in 1862 for Company D, First Kansas Colored Volunteer Infantry Regiment).[17]

## Dissent Within Union Forces

"Once let the black man get upon his person the brass letters U.S.; let him get an eagle on his button, and a musket on his shoulder, and bullets in his pocket, and there is no power on earth or under the earth which can deny that he has earned the right of citizenship in the United States."

Frederick Douglass[18]

Not everyone shared in the views that were expressed by Douglass, nor did all of Lincoln's generals support his new policy of protection within the Union lines for contrabands and the use of Negro men as soldiers. On March 31, 1863, Major General Henry W. Halleck sent a warning to Major General U.S. Grant concerning uses and treatment of Negroes:

GENERAL: ...Every slave withdrawn from the enemy is equivalent to a white man put *hors de combat*.

Again, it is the policy of the Government to use the Negroes of the South, as far as practicable, as a military force, for the defense of forts, depots, &c.... In the hands of the enemy, they (Negroes) are used with much effect against us; in our hands, we must try to use them with the best possible effect against the rebels.

It has been reported to the Secretary of War that many of the officers of your command not only discourage the negroes from coming under our protection, but by ill-treatment force them to return to their masters. This is not only bad policy in itself, but is directly opposed to the policy adopted by the Government. Whatever may be the individual opinion of an officer in regard to the wisdom of measures so adopted and announced by the Government, it is the duty of every one to cheerfully and honestly endeavor to carry out the measures so adopted....

It is expected that you will use your official and personal influence to remove prejudices on this subject, and to fully and thoroughly carry out the policy now adopted and ordered by the Government....

The character of the war has very much changed within the last year. There is now no possible hope of reconciliation with the rebels. The Union party in the South is virtually destroyed. There can be no peace but that which is forced by the sword. We must conquer the slave oligarchy or become slaves ourselves—the manufacturers mere "hewers of wood and drawers of water" to Southern aristocrats.[19]

By the time the first companies of the Fifty-fourth Massachusetts Volunteer Infantry Regiment under Colonel Robert G. Shaw (the regiment on which the motion picture *Glory* was based) were raised, the War Department had moved

*Alfred R. Waud's 1866* Harper's Weekly *drawing shows black infantrymen mustering out at Little Rock. (Courtesy of Ronnie A. Nichols)*

to organize Negro troops on a regular basis. In March 1863, Adjutant General Lorenzo Thomas was dispatched from Washington, D.C., to the Mississippi River Valley to raise as many troops of African descent, led by white officers, as possible. He also had instructions to ensure that the Union generals carried out the president's policies. On April 6, 1863, General Thomas addressed seven thousand white Union soldiers at Fort Curtis in Helena, Arkansas. He would report that the "policy respecting the blacks was most enthusiastically received."[20]

The most important questions concerned the responses of the newly freed black men. Would they join the Yankee army? Would they run or would they fight? And what would be the reaction of the Confederacy when black men were encountered on the field of battle?

By December 1863, Thomas had organized twenty-nine regiments of troops of African descent with an aggregate strength of 20,830. These men had been recruited from the black population of the six Southern and border states of Alabama, Arkansas, Louisiana, Mississippi, Missouri, and Tennessee.[21] Arkansas was credited with 5,526 black men in the Union army. An aggregate number of black men serving in the Union army by the end of the Civil War was 178,892, including 7,000 noncommissioned officers. These men made up between nine and ten percent of the Federal army. A total of 166 all-black regiments were raised: 145 infantry, 7 cavalry, 12 heavy artillery, 1 light artillery and 1 engineer.[22]

Black soldiers in the Union army would serve in battles at Milliken's Bend, Port Hudson, Morris Island, Honey Springs, Nashville, and James River, among many others. All together, they fought in 449 battles, including 39 major engagements.

The army utilized the majority of these black units for heavy fatigue duty. They endured poor camp locations, insufficient medical care, inferior weapons, and lower pay than white Federal soldiers; they sometimes faced racism from their white

officers. (By April of 1864, the Department of United States
Colored Troops—U.S.C.T.—was established in all locales where
these troops were serving to address these issues.) The death toll
in the black regiments was high—more than thirty-seven
percent, or 68,178.[23] Many died from disease and abusive labor
or fatigue duties, coupled in some cases with inadequately
trained medical personnel. On the battlefield the proportion of
black soldiers killed was higher than that of their white comrades. And if they suffered the misfortune of being captured,
the penalty for a black soldier was far greater than for a white
Yankee. Black men armed with rifles had raised fears in the
South of a mass slave rebellion, and the Confederate States of
America viewed arming of black men as insurrectionary.

Responding to this longstanding slave-owner fear,
Confederate president Jefferson Davis in December 1862 issued
a proclamation declaring that U.S. General Benjamin F. Butler
was a felon deserving of capital punishment. Davis decreed the
terms of punishment, writing "by virtue of my authority as
Commander-in-Chief of the Armies of the Confederate States":

- That all Negro slaves captured in arms be at once delivered over to
  the executive authorities of the respective States to which they
  belong to be dealt with according to the laws of said States.
- That the like orders be executed in all cases with respect to all commissioned officers of the United States when found serving in
  company with armed slaves in insurrection against the authorities of
  the different States of this Confederacy.[24]

In another case, Lieutenant General E. Kirby Smith, commanding Confederate forces in the Trans-Mississippi West,
ordered that Negro troops and their white officers be given no
quarter. An early example of this type of behavior occurred at
Milliken's Bend, Louisiana, June 7, 1863. When Lieutenant
General Smith was informed that black prisoners had been
taken, he wrote to Major General Richard Taylor, commander

of the District of Western Louisiana, that "I hope this may not be so, and that your subordinates...may have recognized the propriety of giving no quarter to Negroes and their officers." Union General U.S. Grant later received a report that there had been a mass hanging of black soldiers after the battle at Milliken's Bend.[25]

The First Kansas Colored fell prey to the "no quarter" policy prior to the events at Milliken's Bend. On May 18, 1863, a foraging party made up of twenty-five men from the First Kansas Colored and twenty men from the white Second Kansas Battery were attacked near Sherwood, Missouri. Colonel James Williams would give this account a day later: "I visited the scene of this engagement the morning after its occurrence...and for the first time beheld the horrible evidences of the demoniac spirit of these rebel fiends in their treatment of our dead and wounded. Men were found with their brains beaten out with clubs, and the bloody weapons left by their sides, and their bodies were most horribly mutilated."[26]

## Poison Spring

I went into action with about 450 enlisted men and 13 officers of the line. Seven out of that gallant 13 were killed or wounded...One hundred seventeen men are killed and 67 wounded, some of them mortally.
Major Richard G. Ward
First Kansas Colored
April 20, 1864
[In the Field, Camden][27]

The Rebel victors on the field at Poison Spring taunted the wounded and dying as they carried out the "no quarter" policy: "Where are the First Niggers now? Cut to pieces—gone to hell—due to poor management!"[28] There had been poor management in the Union command that decided the fate of the First Kansas Colored (later designated the Seventy-ninth United States Colored Volunteer Infantry Regiment). However, the poor management was not the design of Colonel James Williams and the officers of the First Kansas.

General Frederick Steele left Little Rock with his troops ill prepared in terms of rations for such an expedition as the Red River Campaign. General Steele sent the First Kansas Colored out on April 17, 1864, as part of a foraging detail with 198 wagons to be filled. The military escort was probably under-sized for a wagon train of this size in enemy territory. On the eighteenth of April, the First Kansas and the rest of the foraging party were attacked by Confederate artillery (two batteries) joined by musketry fire. Steele sat in Camden—within earshot of the events that were being carried against Federal troops. Yet he did not respond in time to save the day, nor the lives of many of his brave Negro troops.[29] On May 21, 1864, the Fort Smith newspaper, *The New Era*, reported:

> "We have it from reliable sources that Gen. Thayer repeatedly asked permission to sally out with his Division to cover the retreat of the devoted little band, but to no avail."

Just before the end of America's Civil War—a war to pre-serve the Union, a war for States Rights, a war that was not about slavery, a war that did not need any help from the darker brother—Confederate president Jefferson Davis signed a bill on March 13, 1865, authorizing the use of Negro slaves as sol-diers in the Confederate Army. Meanwhile, on April 3, the all-black U.S. Second Division of the Twenty-fifth Corps helped chase Confederate General Robert E. Lee's army from Petersburg to Appomattox Court House. The combined black and white Union soldiers were advancing on General Lee's trapped army with fixed bayonets when the Confederate troops surrendered.[30]

What if the Confederacy had taken up the request of a Helena citizen to use black troops in 1861? What if the Southern states had tapped their natural resources—the people of African descent? What if Confederate general and former Helena resident Patrick R. Cleburne had succeeded in his plan to save the Confederacy by utilizing black men as soldiers, instead of being ridiculed for such an unpatriotic plan?

The faithful service and sacrifice of these men of African descent earned them the right to be called African Americans, for they helped forge the Thirteenth, Fourteenth, and Fifteenth amendments to the United States Constitution, which abolished slavery and established the rights to equal protection of the laws, the rights of citizenship, and the right to vote—as Americans.

≈

1. Dudley Taylor Cornish, *The Sable Arm: Negro Troops in the Union Army, 1861-1865* (New York: W.W. Norton, 1956), 4.

2. Crispus Attucks, a black man, the first martyr of the American Revolution, was killed March 5, 1770, in Boston, Massachusetts. Robert Ewell Greene, *Black Defenders of America, 1775-1973* (Chicago: Johnson Publishing Company, 1974), 3-12. Blacks were held as slaves in all thirteen colonies. During the Revolution, one of six Americans was black, and ninety-nine percent of blacks in America were slaves. Originally they fought under a substitute system, which permitted a white man to send his slave rather than go himself. Later Congress not only approved their enlistment, but called for the reenlistment of blacks. By 1779, fifteen percent of the Continental army was black, usually as service troops building defenses, but often as line soldiers. By the end of the Revolution, several states had abolished slavery and others gradually voted to emancipate their slaves. Mike Wright, *What They Didn't Teach About the American Revolution* (Novato, Calif.: Presido Press, Inc., 2001), 233-234.

3. John Hope Franklin, and Genna Rae McNeil, *African Americans and The Living Constitution* (Washington, D.C., Smithsonian Institution Press, 1995), 23.

4. *African Americans: Voices of Triumph–Perseverance* (Alexandria, Va.: Time-Life Custom Publishing, 1993), 90-93.

5. Lerone Bennett, Jr., *Before the Mayflower: A History of Black America* (New York: Penguin Books, 1962), 178. Dred Scott, a Missouri slave, had been taken to Illinois by his master and then to a fort in the northern part of the Louisiana Purchase, which had been designated as free territory by the Missouri Compromise. Chief Justice Roger B. Taney, a Maryland slaveholder, said that since the Missouri Compromise was unconstitutional, masters could take their slaves into free states and continue to own them. The net effect of all this was the de facto nationalization of the slave system.

6. U.S. War Department, *The War of the Rebellion: A Compilation of the Official Records of the Union and Confederate Armies*, series IV, vol. I (Washington, D.C.: Government Printing Office, 1900), 482 (hereafter cited as *Official Records*).

7. *Official Records*, 529.

8. Noah Andre Trudeau, *Like Men of War: Black Troops in the Civil War 1862-1865* (New York: Little, Brown and Company, 1998), 7.

9. Benjamin Quarles, *Lincoln and The Negro* (New York: Oxford University Press, 1992), 153.

10. Long, *The Civil War Day by Day*, 700-702.

11. Orville W. Taylor, *Negro Slavery in Arkansas* (Durham, N.C.: Duke University Press, 1958), 125.

12. Carl H. Moneyhon, *The Impact of the Civil War and Reconstruction on Arkansas* (Baton Rouge: Louisiana State University Press, 1994), 14.

13. Molefi K. Asante and Mark T. Mattson *Historical and Cultural Atlas of African Americans* (New York: Macmillan Publishing Company, 1992), 80.

14. *U.S. Statutes at Large: Treaties and Proclamations of the United States of America*, vol. 12 (Boston: Little, Brown, 1863), 589-92.

15. "Shortly after the attack on Fort Sumter in April 1861, approximately 1,500 free men of African descent gathered in New Orleans to show support in defense of their homeland. They organized themselves into a regiment called the 'Native

Guards,' which Governor Thomas O. Moore accepted into the Louisiana Militia on May 2nd." C.P. Weaver, *Thank God My Regiment an African One* (Baton Rouge: Louisiana State University Press, 1998), 4.

16. *Official Records*, series I, vol. XII, 525.

17. Trudeau, 20. On March 17, 1890, in Washington, D.C., James M. Williams, late colonel of the First Kansas Colored Volunteers and brevet brigadier general of volunteers, testified before the Committee on War Claims. Colonel William spoke on behalf of Captain William D. Matthews.

> (House Report No. 889. Fifty-first Congress, first session, published in *Report of the Adjutant General of the State of Kansas, 1861-1865*, Vol. 1 (Topeka: Kansas State Printing Co., 1896)

> The Committee on War Claims, to whom was referred the bill (H.R. 7242) for the relief of William D. Matthews, report as follows:

> It appears from the records of the War Department that William D. Matthews recruited a company of 81 men from August 17, 1862, to November 25, 1862, for an organization known as the First Regiment Kansas Colored Volunteers.... Thirty-seven of the men recruited by William D. Matthews appear on the rolls of the reorganized regiment. [Matthews was not appointed or mustered into service as an officer of the regiment. Why he was not mustered in is not disclosed by the records of the War Department.]

> [W]ith instruction to recruit and organize companies and parts of companies for said service, and among the recruiting officers so appointed was William D. Matthews, a colored man of recognized ability and influence, this appointment being made with the understanding that when the regiment was organized, that said William D. Matthews would be mustered in as an officer....

> By reason of the failure of orders to the mustering officers the regimental organization was not completed until the 2nd day of May, 1863, when it was mustered into the service as the First Kansas Colored Volunteers. On being mustered into the service the mustering officer refused to muster said William D. Matthews, assigning as a reason that he could not muster a person of African descent as an officer....

> In view of the above recited facts, as an act of long-delayed justice, I respectfully but urgently request your honorable committee recommend that said William D. Matthews be paid an amount equal to the pay and allowances of a captain of infantry from the 4th day of August, 1862 to the 2nd day of May 1863.

William D. Matthews would serve again during the Civil War as recruiting officer and second lieutenant of the all-black Independent Battery U.S. Colored Light Artillery, along with Captain H. Ford Douglas (Douglas had served in the all-white ninety-fifth Illinois, Company G).

18. Benjamin Quarles, *The Negro in the Civil War* (Boston: Little, Brown, 1969), 184.

19. Joseph T. Glatthaar, *Forged in Battle: The Civil War Alliance of Black Soldiers and White Officers* (New York: The Free Press, 1990), 29.

20. Quarles, *The Negro in the Civil War*, 194.

21. Cornish, 250.

22. Long, 708.

23. Leslie H. Fishel, Jr., and Benjamin Quarles, *The Black American: A Documentary History* (Glenview, Ill.: Scott, Foresman and Co., 1978), 217.

24. *Official Records*, series 2, vol. 5, 796-7.

25. Cornish, 168. Admiral David D. Porter reported to Grant on June 7 that "The enemy attacked at Milliken's Bend; commenced driving the Negro regiments, and killed all they captured. This infuriated the Negroes, who turned on the rebels and slaughtered them like sheep." *Official Records*, series XXXVI, vol. XVIV, part 2, 453. Charles A. Dana, a special commissioner of the War Department, reported on June 21 that "Porter reports to General Grant...that 5 or 6 Federal prisoners, black and white, captured by the rebels in the recent fight at Milliken's Bend, were hanged at Delhi in the presence of General Taylor and his staff..." *OR*, S XXXVI, vol. XXIV, part 1, 105.

26. Trudeau, 103-104.

27. Ibid., 194.

28. Glenn L. Carle, "The First Kansas Colored," *American Heritage*, vol. XLIII, no. 1 (Feb./March 1992), 90-91.

29. Gregory J.W. Urwin, "Massacre at Poison Springs," *North & South* vol. 3, no. 6, August 2000, 53.

30. Bennett, 473.

# The First Kansas Colored
## at Honey Springs

### Frank Arey

Poison Spring was not the first engagement between the First Kansas Colored Volunteer Infantry Regiment and some of its Confederate foes. Earlier, at the Battle of Honey Springs on July 17, 1863, the Federal First Kansas Colored fought the Confederate Twenty-ninth Texas Cavalry Regiment and the First Choctaw Regiment (also known as the First Choctaw and Chickasaw Regiment). A study of the combat between these units at Honey Springs, Indian Territory, provides some context for understanding the events at Poison Spring. This survey briefly summarizes the action at Honey Springs and then gives greater attention to the combat between the First Kansas Colored, the Twenty-ninth Texas Cavalry, and the First Choctaw. It concludes by examining possible explanations for the treatment of the First Kansas Colored at Poison Spring.[1]

The Battle of Honey Springs took place twenty-five miles south of Fort Gibson along the old Texas Road, where it crosses Elk Creek; the main action occurred just north of the crossing. The settlement of Honey Springs, some two miles south of the crossing at Elk Creek, was the site of a Confederate supply depot. On the Federal side, Major General James G. Blunt commanded a force of less than three thousand men. Confederate Brigadier General Douglas H. Cooper unofficially reported that he had "only 2,000 effective men in his camp," but that estimate may be too conservative. On the other hand,

Blunt's estimate of six thousand Confederates appears to be somewhat high.[2]

Cooper deployed his force to cover the Texas Road bridge over Elk Creek, as well as fords upstream and downstream. Three Texas cavalry regiments, all fighting dismounted, and a battery of light howitzers protected the Texas Road crossing; one of these cavalry units was the Twenty-ninth Texas Cavalry, positioned in the center of the Confederate line astride the Texas Road. Cooper intended to hold the First Choctaw in reserve at its camp near Honey Springs.[3]

Blunt's Federal soldiers approached the area after an overnight march; he gave his men a brief two-hour respite while he and his staff prepared a plan of attack. At approximately ten o'clock in the morning, the Federal force moved down the Texas Road in two columns. When they were one quarter of a mile north of the Confederate line, the left-hand column deployed in a line to the left of the road, while the right-hand column deployed into a line to the right of the road. The First Kansas Colored marched and deployed in the right-hand column.[4]

A fight of approximately two hours length ensued on the north side of Elk Creek. Blunt made good use of the Federal superiority in artillery—he had twelve pieces of artillery on the field to Cooper's four. A supply of defective gunpowder further weakened the Confederate defense; at least one of the Texas regiments was forced to use its muskets as clubs due to the condition of its powder. Eventually, the Confederate center began to give way, and the entire Confederate line withdrew. Cooper conducted a fighting retreat with his cavalry, but the Federal force nonetheless captured his supply depot and drove the Confederates from the field. Cooper reported Confederate casualties of 134 killed and wounded and 47 captured; a revised statement lists Federal casualties of 13 killed and 62 wounded.[5]

The First Kansas Colored played a conspicuous part in the Battle of Honey Springs. The regiment had already seen action in the Indian Territory at the First Battle of Cabin Creek on July 1–2, 1863, when it helped to repulse a Confederate attack on a Federal supply train bound for Fort Gibson. A Federal cavalry-man spoke to members of the First Kansas Colored after the supply train reached Fort Gibson, just before the action at Honey Springs.

> I have talked with some of the colored soldiers, and they seem anxious to meet the enemy on an open field....These colored soldiers say that they have heard that the enemy are furious for the blood of those negroes who have gone into the "Yankee" service, and that they have come down here to give the rebels an opportunity of satiating them-selves with their blood. But they are convinced that there will be as much rebel as negro blood spilt....

The Confederates had different expectations. One of the officers in the Twenty-ninth Texas Cavalry had a slave present before Honey Springs; the slave "frequently heard the Southern officers, talking with each other, say that they did not believe colored soldiers would fight, and that all the Southern troops would have to do would be to march up to the colored men and take them in."[6]

After reaching the battlefield on the morning of July 17, 1863, the First Kansas Colored enjoyed its two-hour rest along with the remainder of Blunt's Federal troops. Captain Ethan Earle of Company F, First Kansas Colored, recalled marching to the battlefield "in a very severe rain storm, which lasted till eight o'clock in the morning." During the rest the men "found about one cracker to a man" for their breakfast. "By this time the rain had ceased, the sun came out clear, and we were all dry and the weather warm, so that we had as good a fighting day as could be made, free from dust."[7]

The First Kansas Colored advanced with the rest of Blunt's force at ten o'clock; the regiment was in the right-hand column that advanced south down the Texas Road to within one quarter

of a mile from the Confederate line. At that point the First
Kansas Colored deployed into line to the right of the road in
support of Captain E.A. Smith's Second Kansas Battery, which
commenced shelling the Confederate forces. As the Federal
troops deployed, they came under fire from the lone
Confederate battery on the field. While some damage was
inflicted on the Federal batteries, Earle recalled that "[a]t first
the enemy shot very wild and our men paid no attention to
it...."[8]

Deployed across the field from the First Kansas Colored was
the Twenty-ninth Texas Cavalry and another Texas cavalry regiment, both fighting dismounted. Lieutenant Colonel Otis G.
Welch of the Twenty-ninth Texas Cavalry reported that "[t]he
whole space in front of us was covered with small bushes, which
concealed our position and almost masked the approach of the
enemy." Similarly, Blunt recalled that "[t]heir position was...in
the edge of the timber, which served as a cover, while we were
compelled to advance over the open prairie." However, as Earle
noted, this position would prove disadvantageous to the Texans:
"Two Texas Regiments were stationed opposite our colored
Regiment, their intention was to annihilate us, they used
double barrel shotguns, which in the timber and thick brush
were not very effective."[9]

Blunt pushed his artillery and supporting line of infantry
forward from their initial positions. The artillery advanced to
within three hundred yards of the Confederate line, exchanging
fire with the Confederate howitzers. The First Kansas Colored
moved forward to support Smith's battery, under direct orders
from Blunt to "keep an eye to those guns of the enemy, and take
them at the point of the bayonet, if an opportunity offers."
Colonel James M. Williams of the First Kansas Colored ordered
his men to "fix bayonets" and then moved the regiment to the
right of Smith's battery, which continued to hammer away at
the Confederate line.[10]

The Twenty-ninth Texas Cavalry stood its ground as the Federal line approached. Welch reported that a Federal "battery to the left of us, also one in front, complimented us occasionally with shot and shell, though the heaviest fire was directed to the right. A constant fire was kept up by the skirmishers on both sides." At some point during this period, the skirmishers of the Twenty-ninth Texas Cavalry were driven in. However, with the exception of their howitzers, the main Confederate line had not yet opened fire, so that its exact location in the timber and brush was not certain to the advancing Federals.[11]

At last Smith's battery ceased firing, whereupon "our gallant colonel [Williams] gave the command 'forward,' and every man [of the First Kansas Colored] stepped promptly and firmly in his place, advancing in good order" with the remainder of the Federal line. The regiment advanced to approximately forty yards' distance from the Confederate dismounted cavalrymen, halting on the right of another Federal unit, the Second Colorado Volunteer Infantry Regiment. Up to this point both sides held their fire.

> Colonel Williams then gave the command, "Ready, aim, fire," and immediately there went forth two long lines of smoke and flame, the one from the enemy putting forth at the same instant, as if mistaking the command as intended for themselves, or as a demonstration of their willingness to meet us promptly.

On the Confederate side, Welch reported a similar scene: "The enemy advanced in line of battle four deep along our entire front....We reserved our fire until the enemy had approached within twenty yards, and then poured upon them a galling fire."[12]

A close-range firefight ensued between the opposing lines; Earle recalled that "[t]his action was sharp and pointed for an hour," with both sides inflicting casualties at such a short range.

The first Confederate volley killed Williams's horse, and severely wounded the colonel in the chest, face, and hands. Likewise, Federal fire wounded Colonel Charles DeMorse, commander of the Twenty-ninth Texas, in the arm. The firefight continued unabated.[13]

Units became intermingled in the fighting; this was caused by the close proximity of the combatants, the poor visibility in the brush and timber, and the smoke and confusion that normally accompanied combat. On the left of the First Kansas Colored, a detachment of the Second Colorado advanced too far into the Confederate lines and was almost surrounded and captured. A force from the First

*Colonel Charles DeMorse of the Twenty-ninth Texas Cavalry was wounded at the Battle of Honey Springs. He and his men would face the First Kansas Colored Infantry Regiment again at Poison Spring, Arkansas. (Courtesy of the Confederate Research Center, Hill College, Hillsboro, Texas)*

Kansas Colored's left wing moved to rescue the detachment, "which they very quickly effected" by driving off the Confederates with several volleys, thereby earning the respect and gratitude of the Second Colorado.[14]

An even more dramatic situation involving the Twenty-ninth Texas Cavalry unfolded on the right wing of the First Kansas Colored. After Williams was wounded and left the field, command of the First Kansas Colored passed to Lieutenant Colonel John Bowles, who was stationed on the unit's right. He reported:

[O]n the extreme right...some of our Indians had ridden in the brush between us and the enemy. I immediately ordered them to fall back, and to the right. The enemy, which has since proven to have been the Twenty-ninth Texas Regiment...supposed from the command that we were giving way in front, and, like true soldiers, commenced to press, as they supposed, a retreating foe. They advanced to within 25 paces, when they were met by a volley of musketry that sent them back in great confusion and disorder. Their color-bearer fell, but the colors were immediately raised, and again promptly shot down. A second time they were raised, and again I caused a volley to be fired upon them, when they were left by the enemy as a trophy to our well-directed musketry.[15]

Throughout the firefight the Federal line continued to move forward. Blunt stated that his "men steadily advanced into the edge of the timber, and the fighting was unremitting and terrific for two hours...." After repulsing the Twenty-ninth Texas Cavalry, the right wing of the First Kansas Colored "press[ed] the enemy back to a cornfield, where he broke and fled in confusion."[16]

The Confederate line finally yielded to the Federal attack. Cooper, returning from an attempt to summon reinforcements for the Confederate troops in the center, encountered evidence of the Federal advance. "Riding back near the creek, I discovered our men in small parties giving way. These increased until the retreat became general." The battery and Texas cavalrymen in the Confederate center withdrew across Elk Creek, fighting as they went across the bridge and south to Honey Springs.[17]

The withdrawal of the Twenty-ninth Texas Cavalry reflected the confusion on the battlefield. While his men continued their firefight with the Federal infantry, Welch noticed that "the whole right had given away, and we were fast being flanked on our right and left." When the right wing of the Twenty-ninth Texas Cavalry heard an order to fall back given to the Twentieth Texas Cavalry, the right wing of the Twenty-ninth decided to fall back, too; Welch's men on the left of the regiment held their ground. Shortly thereafter, Welch pulled his men back to a small branch of the creek. He then discovered that "all on our right had given

away and that the enemy were passing rapidly to our rear...."
Somehow Welch managed to march his men in the opposite
direction, up Elk Creek; they evaded the Federal army and
rejoined Cooper's command after camping apart overnight.[18]

The First Kansas Colored initially fell back to the battlefield
after helping to break the Confederate line. A Federal unit on
its right, the Second Indian Home Guard Regiment, moved
forward to take up the pursuit; its commander notified Bowles
in an attempt to prevent the First Kansas Colored from mis-
taking his men for Confederates. As the Second Indian Home
Guard moved to the front, some of its men decided to take
advantage of the First Kansas Colored's hard work, as Bowles
explained in his report.

> Some of [the Second Indian Home Guard] passed to our front and
> carried off the colors we had three times shot down and driven the
> enemy from in defeat and loss. Some of my officers and men shouted out
> in remonstrance, and asked permission to break ranks and get them. I
> refused permission, and told them the matter could be righted hereafter.

Apparently the matter was not that easily resolved. In his
official report, the commander of the Second Indian Home
Guard claimed "[a] stand of colors was captured by my men,"
and the incident was still the source of controversy thereafter.[19]

In Cooper's words, the Confederate "forces were now in full
retreat and the enemy pressing them closely." While some elements of the Federal force remained on or near the battlefield,
other units continued the pursuit. Cooper burned his supplies
stored at Honey Springs and called on his reserves to conduct a
series of holding actions, while those Confederate units with-
drawing from the fight escorted his trains to safety. One of these
reserve units, of course, was the First Choctaw Regiment.[20]

Although meant to stay in reserve all day, the First Choctaw
had in fact been on the move for much of the fight. Cooper

ordered the regiment to remain near Honey Springs, while "sending pickets out on the road across the mountain in the direction of Prairie Springs." Colonel Tandy Walker, commander of the First Choctaw, misunderstood these orders; he took

the entire regiment, less a portion previously ordered to the front, on this mission to Prairie Springs. Summoned by messengers to return, Walker's force missed the fight for the bridge at Elk Creek and the first holding action of other elements of the reserves.[21]

Blunt's troops continued to exploit their victory. Captain Henry Hopkins's Kansas Battery went into position south of Elk Creek and drove off one Confederate covering force with artillery fire. Limbering up, the battery moved on another quarter of a mile, when a line of Confederate cavalry caused the battery to deploy a second

*Brigadier General Douglas Cooper led Confederate troops to defeat at Honey Springs. (Courtesy of the Oklahoma Historical Society)*

time. The First Kansas Colored also participated in the pursuit after its pause at the battlefield. Earle remembered that the Confederates "at every creek or piece of timber and brush would make a stand with an attempt to check our pursuit; this they did three times during the day...."[22]

At this point, the First Choctaw reappeared in response to Cooper's messages; from the accounts, it is likely that this unit was the force of Confederate cavalry that caused the second deployment of Hopkins's battery. There is a strong possibility that the First Choctaw and the First Kansas Colored made some contact at this point. Cooper described the action from the Confederate perspective:

> The Choctaws, under Colonel Walker, opportunely arrived at this time, and under my personal direction charged the enemy, who had now planted a battery upon the timbered ridge about 1,000 yards north of Honey Springs. With their usual intrepidity the Choctaws went at them, giving the war-whoop, and succeeded in checking the advance of the enemy until their force could be concentrated and all brought up. The Choctaws, discouraged on account of the worthless ammunition, then gave way, and were ordered to fall back....

The Federal perspective was not that grand. Hopkins reported that the Confederates were "driven back after the firing of a few rounds of shell." Similarly, Bowles reported that the First Kansas Colored advanced "skirmishing occasionally with the enemy."[23]

For all intents and purposes, the Battle of Honey Springs was over. The pursuing Federal units advanced three miles south of Elk Creek, or just a mile south of Honey Springs, and halted their pursuit. Cooper withdrew; although reinforced that evening by three thousand Arkansas cavalrymen commanded by Brigadier General William Cabell, Cooper did not choose to renew the fight. The next day, July 18, 1863, Blunt and his Federal units retired to Fort Gibson.[24]

One other incident at Honey Springs bears upon the subject: the discovery of a supply of handcuffs or shackles at the Confederate supply depot. Colonel Thomas Moonlight, Blunt's chief of staff who participated in the battle and was therefore at the scene, explains:

> [S]ome 500 pairs of shackles were captured, which were designed to be placed upon the limbs of our negro soldiers when Fort Gibson was cap-

tured. The 1st Kansas Colored participated with great gallantry in the fight and grinned from ear to ear at the sight of their old companions the *shackles*.

This story is corroborated by one of Wiley Britton's sources.

David Griffith, a colored man, who was waiting on Major J.A. Carroll, of one of General Cooper's Texas regiments at the time of the battle, and who left him and came to the colored regiment at Fort Smith in September and enlisted in Company G of that regiment and served his time out, stated that he frequently heard Southern officers say that the handcuffs were brought there to be put on colored soldiers they expected to capture.

Needless to say, the handcuffs or shackles were not used for their intended purpose after the battle.[25] Was there anything in this first encounter between the First Kansas Colored, the Twenty-ninth Texas Cavalry, and the First Choctaw that could explain the conduct of these Confederate units at Poison Spring? Did the Federal regiment provoke the treatment it received on April 18, 1864, just over nine months later? Three subjects merit consideration: the conduct of the First Kansas Colored during and after Honey Springs; the captured handcuffs; and the regiment's role in giving the Confederates a score to settle.

Federal officers uniformly praised the conduct of the First Kansas Colored. Blunt singled out only one regiment for special praise in his official report: "The First Kansas (colored) particularly distinguished itself; they fought like veterans.... Their coolness and bravery I have never seen surpassed...." Likewise, the unit behaved itself after the battle. Moonlight recalled: "[B]e it said to the memory of the 1st Kansas Colored they behaved with marked humanity and kindness to the wounded, who but a few hours before had [worked] to place the yoke of slavery for ever on their necks...."[26]

It would be easy to dismiss these comments as history written by the victors, until one considers what the Confederates did not say about the regiment in their writings. Cooper, DeMorse, and Welch did not mention any misbehavior by the First Kansas Colored in their official reports. Colonel Asa Morgan, commanding the Confederate post at Fort Smith, wrote about the battle to his wife, but did not mention any Federal outrages. John Harrell's 1899 history is particularly telling. Harrell was an officer in one of Cabell's units that reinforced Cooper the evening of the battle; Cabell's brigade remained in the area for several days, and Harrell described the battlefield after Blunt withdrew. In his history, Harrell makes no reference to untoward behavior by the First Kansas Colored—and certainly a postwar history would seem to be a good opportunity for an ex-Confederate to mention any Federal atrocities, if they occurred.[27]

These primary sources compel the conclusion that the First Kansas Colored did not misbehave at Honey Springs, either during or after the battle. Federal officers were pleased with the regiment's performance; Confederate officers never mentioned any incidents involving the regiment in their writings, contemporary or otherwise.

The captured handcuffs intended for the men of the First Kansas Colored do not seem to bear on the regiment's subsequent treatment at Poison Spring. Apparently, the regiment did not know about the handcuffs until after the battle was over. Even then, this discovery did not affect the unit's treatment of the Confederate wounded, as demonstrated above. Obviously the handcuffs speak more to the attitudes of the Confederates than to the behavior of the First Kansas Colored. Their presence tends to corroborate the slave's report that the Confederates did not expect the First Kansas Colored to fight.[28]

Finally, there is the fact that a Federal regiment of ex-slaves helped to defeat a Confederate force. One Confederate soldier from the Twentieth Texas Cavalry (dismounted) let his wife know after the battle that Cooper had definitely been beaten.

> We have had a fight with the enemy and they whipped us bad.... I believe they will whip us and whip us all the time until we are rein-forced from Texas or some other point. They are too strong for us...and good fighters. I know it for I have tried them and they are as good as we are, better drilled and better armed.

In fairness to the Confederates, it is difficult to do much with defective gunpowder; Federal artillery outnumbered the Confederate guns three to one; and Blunt concentrated an over-whelming force against the center of an over-extended Confederate line. Regardless, Honey Springs was a Federal victory, and the Confederates knew it.[29]

In light of their expectations, it had to surprise the Confederates that the First Kansas Colored played a role in this Federal win. Instead of simply marching up to the ex-slaves, capturing them, and taking them off in handcuffs and shackles, the Confederates were left with the knowledge that the First Kansas Colored actually fought against them and contributed to their defeat.

For example, there is the issue of the captured Confederate flag. Bowles, who assumed command of the First Kansas Colored after Williams was wounded, reported his regiment's role in taking the flag of one of the Texas regiments, "which has since proven to have been the Twenty-ninth Texas Regiment." There is not complete agreement that the flag belonged to the Twenty-ninth Texas Cavalry. Wiley Britton recorded in his memoirs that the flag belonged to the Twentieth Texas Cavalry; in his later history, he merely referred to "the Texas regiment directly in front" as losing its colors to the First Kansas Colored. Harrell, the Arkansas Confederate officer, claimed in his history that Blunt captured "one stand of Cherokee colors." Moonlight claims that the Federals captured "2 stands of colors," without stating to whom they belonged.[30]

It seems reasonable to accept Bowles's contention that the flag was that of the Twenty-ninth Texas Cavalry, although Cooper, DeMorse, and Welch make no mention of the loss. Britton and Harrell were not present for the battle (even though they spoke directly to participants); Moonlight's account is inconclusive. Bowles was on the ground, directly in the fight, with a motivation to ascertain the true ownership of the colors.

If the flag was that of the Twenty-ninth Texas Cavalry, that provides a possible explanation (although not necessarily the exclusive explanation) for that Confederate unit's treatment of the First Kansas Colored at Poison Spring. As James McPherson explains, the loss of a flag was no small thing to any regiment:

> The most meaningful symbols of regimental pride were the colors—the regimental and national flags, which bonded the men's loyalty to unit, state, and nation. The flags acquired a special mystique for Civil War soldiers....One of the most honorable feats a regiment could accomplish was to capture enemy colors; the worst shame imaginable was to lose its own colors to the enemy.

If the Twenty-ninth Texas Cavalry lost its flag, that alone would be cause for embarrassment and motivation for revenge. Losing the flag due to the efforts of the First Kansas Colored would only add salt to the wound, when one considers that the Confederates did not expect the regiment to fight.[31]

Other aspects of the action possibly left Confederate participants believing they had a score to settle. DeMorse, the commander of the Twenty-ninth Texas Cavalry wounded by Federal fire, never fully recovered from his wound—his arm was disabled for the rest of his life. He later commanded a Confederate cavalry brigade at Poison Spring, which raises the question of whether DeMorse sought revenge against the First Kansas

Colored. Likewise, the First Choctaw's commander, Walker, commanded another Confederate cavalry brigade at Poison Spring—was this an opportunity to avenge the former defeat?[32]

James McPherson identified this notion of vengeance, or revenge, as one of many factors that motivated Civil War soldiers in general, and Texans in particular.

> An essential component of the masculine code of honor was revenge for insult and injury. Hatred of the object of vengeance often accompanied this code…. These sentiments played a stronger role in the motivation of Confederate than of Union soldiers…mainly for the obvious reason that the South suffered so much more death and devastation than the North….
>
> For reasons not entirely clear (the state was scarcely touched by Union invasion), Texans seemed particularly ferocious on this score.

The Twenty-ninth Texas Cavalry, and to a lesser extent the First Choctaw, were arguably motivated by a desire for revenge. Suffering defeat, the loss of a flag, the wounding of DeMorse—all of these things were brought about, in part, by the efforts of the First Kansas Colored. These two Confederate regiments apparently exacted their revenge at Poison Spring.[33]

If the Battle of Honey Springs planted any seed for the bitter harvest at Poison Spring, that seed would seem to be the First Kansas Colored Volunteer Infantry Regiment's role in causing the Confederate defeat. The record fails to suggest any other cause, since the First Kansas Colored did not misbehave at Honey Springs. Of course, there were other Confederate units present at Poison Spring besides the two focused on here; since these other units did not fight at Honey Springs, they may have been motivated by something other than the First Kansas Colored's role at that battle. Similarly, one cannot discount race as a factor in the First Kansas Colored's treatment at Poison Spring. Nonetheless, the encounter at Honey Springs between the three units focused on here does provide some basis for understanding, at least in part, why the First Kansas Colored suffered as it did during and after the action at Poison Spring.

≈

1. Edwin C. Bearss, *Steele's Retreat From Camden* (Little Rock, Ark.: Pioneer Press, 1966; reprint, Little Rock, Ark.: Eagle Press, 1990), 40; General Orders No. 25, 14 July 1863, in United States War Department, *The War of the Rebellion: A Compilation of the Official Records of the Union and Confederate Armies* (Washington, D.C.: GPO, 1888), series 1, vol. 22, part 1: 461-62 (hereafter cited as *Official Records*; all references are to series 1, vol. 22, part 1).

It appears that the Choctaw regiment was also known by other names, such as the First Choctaw and Chickasaw Regiment, or the Chickasaw and Choctaw First Cavalry Regiment. Ibid., 462; Stewart Sifakis, *Compendium of the Confederate Armies: Kentucky, Maryland, Missouri, the Confederate Units and the Indian Units* (New York: Facts on File, 1995), 198-99.

2. Wiley Britton, *Memoirs of the Rebellion on the Border, 1863* (Chicago: Cushing, Thomas & Co., 1882; reprint, Lincoln: University of Nebraska Press, 1993), 355 (hereafter cited as *Memoirs*); James G. Blunt to John M. Schofield, 26 July 1863, Douglas H. Cooper to William Steele, 12 August 1863, *Official Records*, 447-48, 457-62; A.S. Morgan to "My Dear Wife," 21 July 1863, Asa Morgan Letters, Arkansas History Commission, Little Rock, Arkansas (hereafter cited as Morgan Letters).

3. Douglas H. Cooper to William Steele, 12 August 1863, General Orders No. 25, 14 July 1863, *Official Records*, 458-59, 461-62.

4. James G. Blunt to John M. Schofield, 26 July 1863, *Official Records*, 447-48; Thomas Moonlight, "Wartime Reminiscences of Colonel Thomas Moonlight," manuscript transcription of the original in the Yale University Library, Hartford, Connecticut, 27-28 (transcription provided by Kip Lindberg, Springfield, Illinois).

5. James G. Blunt to John M. Schofield, 26 July 1863, Return of Casualties in the Union Forces, undated, Douglas H. Cooper to William Steele, 12 August 1863, *Official Records*, 447-48, 449, 458-60; A.S. Morgan to "My Dear Wife," 21 July 1863, Morgan Letters; J.B. McAfee, comp., *Official Military History of Kansas Regiments* (Leavenworth, Kans.: W.S. Burke, [1870]; reprint, Ottawa, Kans.: Kansas Heritage Press, [1994]), 412.

6. Ibid., 410-12; Britton, *Memoirs*, 316-28, 334; Wiley Britton, *The Civil War on the Border* (New York: G.P. Putnam's Sons, 1899; reprint, Ottawa, Kans.: Kansas Heritage Press, 1994), 2: 123 (hereafter cited as *Civil War on the Border*).

The officer was J.A. Carroll, a major in the Twenty-ninth Texas Cavalry. Ibid.; Stewart Sifakis, *Compendium of the Confederate Armies: Texas* (New York: Facts on File, 1995), 86. See also the text accompanying note 25.

7. Britton, *Civil War on the Border*, 2: 117-18; Ethan Earle, "1st Kansas Colored Vol. Reg't.," 1863-1865," Manuscript, R. Stanton Avery Special Collections Department, New England Historic Genealogical Society, Boston, Massachusetts, 38, 40 (transcription provided by Fort Scott National Historic Site, Fort Scott, Kansas).

8. James G. Blunt to John M. Schofield, 26 July 1863, John Bowles to William R. Judson, 20 July 1863, *Official Records*, 447-48, 449; Britton, *Civil War on the Border*, 2: 118-20; Earle, 40.

9. McAfee, 412; John Bowles to William R. Judson, 20 July 1863, *Official Records*, 450; Otis G. Welch to Thomas Coke Bass, 25 July 1863, Janet B. Hewitt, Noah

Andre Trudeau, Bryce A. Suderow, eds., *Supplement to the Official Records of the Union and Confederate Armies* (Wilmington, N.C.: Broadfoot Publishing Co., 1995), part 1, vol. 4: 149 (hereafter cited as *Supplement OR*; all references are to part 1, vol. 4); James G. Blunt, "General Blunt's Account of His Civil War Experiences," *Kansas Historical Quarterly* 1, no. 3 (May 1932): 244; Earle, 41.

10. John Bowles to William R. Judson, 20 July 1863, E.A. Smith to William R. Judson, 19 July 1863, *Official Records*, 449, 454.

11. Otis G. Welch to Thomas Coke Bass, 25 July 1863, *Supplement OR*, 149; John Bowles to William R. Judson, 20 July 1863, *Official Records*, 449; Britton, *Civil War on the Border*, 2: 120.

12. John Bowles to William R. Judson, 20 July 1863, E.A. Smith to William R. Judson, 19 July 1863, *Official Records*, 449-50, 454; Otis G. Welch to Thomas Coke Bass, 25 July 1863, *Supplement OR*, 149; Britton, *Civil War on the Border*, 2: 120; Moonlight, 28.

13. Britton, *Civil War on the Border*, 2: 120; Earle, 41; John Bowles to William R. Judson, 20 July 1863, *Official Records*, 450; Otis G. Welch to Thomas Coke Bass, 25 July 1863, *Supplement OR*, 150.

14. Britton, *Civil War on the Border*, 2: 121-22; Earle, 43.

15. John Bowles to William R. Judson, 20 July 1863, *Official Records*, 450; Britton, *Civil War on the Border*, 2: 120-21.

16. James G. Blunt to John M. Schofield, 26 July 1863, John Bowles to William R. Judson, 20 July 1863, W.T. Campbell to William R. Judson, 19 July 1863, *Official Records*, 448, 450, 452-53; Moonlight, 28.

17. James G. Blunt to John M. Schofield, 26 July 1863, Douglas H. Cooper to William Steele, 12 August 1863, *Official Records*, 448, 459; Britton, *Civil War on the Border*, 2: 122.

18. Charles DeMorse to Douglas Hancock Cooper, 29 August 1863, Otis G. Welch to Thomas Coke Bass, 25 July 1863, *Supplement OR*, 146-47, 149; Douglas H. Cooper to William Steele, 12 August 1863, *Official Records*, 459-60.

19. John Bowles to William R. Judson, 20 July 1863, Frederick W. Schaurte to Acting Assistant Adjutant General, 20 July 1863, *Official Records*, 450, 451; Britton, *Memoirs*, 361-62.

20. John Bowles to William R. Judson, 20 July 1863, E.A. Smith to William R. Judson, 19 July 1863, Douglas H. Cooper to William Steele, 12 August 1863, *Official Records*, 450, 454, 459-60.

21. Douglas H. Cooper to William Steele, 12 August 1863, General Orders No. 25, 14 July 1863, *Official Records*, 458-60, 462.

22. John Bowles to William R. Judson, 20 July 1863, Henry Hopkins to William A. Phillips, 21 July 1863, *Official Records*, 450, 456-57; Earle, 41.

23. John Bowles to William R. Judson, 20 July 1863, Henry Hopkins to William A. Phillips, 21 July 1863, Douglas H. Cooper to William Steele, 12 August 1863, *Official Records*, 450, 456-57, 460.

24. James G. Blunt to John M. Schofield, 26 July 1863, Frederick W. Schaurte to Acting Assistant Adjutant General, 20 July 1863, *Official Records*, 448, 451; Britton, *Civil War on the Border*, 2: 124-25; John M. Harrell, *Confederate Military History*

*Extended Edition*, vol. 14, *Arkansas*, ed. Clement A. Evans (n.p.: Confederate Publishing Co., 1899; reprint, Wilmington, N.C.: Broadfoot Publishing Co., 1988), 199-201.

25. Moonlight, 28; Britton, *Civil War on the Border*, 2: 123.

26. James G. Blunt to John M. Schofield, 26 July 1863, *Official Records*, 448; Moonlight, 28; Britton, *Civil War on the Border*, 2: 123-24.

27. Douglas H. Cooper to William Steele, 12 August 1863, *Official Records*, 457-61; Charles DeMorse to Douglas Hancock Cooper, 29 August 1863, Otis G. Welch to Thomas Coke Bass, 25 July 1863, *Supplement OR*, 146-47, 148-50; A.S. Morgan to "My Dear Wife," 21 July 1863, Morgan Letters; Harrell, 200-202.

Interestingly, the Texas volume that is the companion to Harrell's Arkansas volume in the *Confederate Military History* series also fails to mention any atrocities at Honey Springs, committed by the First Kansas Colored or otherwise. O.M. Roberts, *Confederate Military History Extended Edition*, vol. 15, *Texas*, ed. Clement A. Evans (n.p.: Confederate Publishing Co., 1899; reprint, Wilmington, N.C.: Broadfoot Publishing Co., 1989), 193-94.

28. Britton, *Civil War on the Border*, 2: 123.

29. R. McDermott to "Dear Wife," 22 July 1863, Vertical File of the Twentieth Texas Cavalry, Harold B. Simpson Hill College History Complex, Hillsboro, Texas; A.S. Morgan to "My Dear Wife," 21 July 1863, Morgan Letters.

30. John Bowles to William R. Judson, 20 July 1863, *Official Records*, 450; Britton, *Memoirs*, 361-62; Britton, *Civil War on the Border*, 2: 120-21; Harrell, 201; Moonlight, 28.

31. James M. McPherson, *For Cause and Comrades: Why Men Fought in the Civil War* (New York: Oxford University Press, 1997), 84.

32. Ernest Wallace, *Charles DeMorse: Pioneer Editor and Statesman* (Lubbock, Tex.: Texas Tech Press, 1943), 147; Bearss, 40.

33. McPherson, 148-49; Gregory J.W. Urwin, "'We Cannot Treat Negroes…as Prisoners of War': Racial Atrocities and Reprisals in Civil War Arkansas," in *Civil War Arkansas: Beyond Battles and Leaders*, eds. Anne J. Bailey and Daniel E. Sutherland (Fayetteville, Ark.: University of Arkansas Press, 2000), 216-17, 223.

# Who Wrote the Poison Spring Letter?

## Mark K. Christ

The letter in the Old State House Museum's Spence Family Collection that inspired the seminar entitled "'I Have Seen Enough Myself…': The Battle of Poison Spring" provides stark testimony to the aftermath of the action of April 18, 1864. The original letter is partially torn, and the missing portion unfortunately includes the signature of the author. This essay will explore available evidence to identify the letter's probable author.

While the battle of Poison Spring and the issues surrounding the treatment of the African-American soldiers killed there are discussed at length in the other essays in this volume, this letter provides an eyewitness account from a Southern soldier who was present on the field at the time the atrocities were committed. The letter proves chillingly personal in that the author recognized several of the black soldiers of the First Kansas Colored Infantry Regiment as former slaves he knew from home. The fragmentary information at the end of the letter gives credence to the anger of Confederate soldiers at Poison Spring on seeing the personal items looted from the area mixed with the seized corn in the unfortunate wagon train.

The text of the letter follows:

Camp 9 miles E of Camden
Ouachita Co April 20th

Dear Sallie,

Its now night and have just learned that a Mr. Moore would start home in the morning soon, so I write by the fire light. We have been annoying the Feds ever since leaving Arkadelphia. The day after I wrote you last, we were (that is, our Co) marched up in the Prairie to support a battery. No one in the Co hurt, one man killed and few wounded near us, some fifty yards off. The cannon balls would strike the ground in front of us and bound over the company. Could see them for a hundred yds before they struck the ground. The Feds the night after moved in direction of Camden and now occupy the place with a large force, the number I have had no reliable means of ascertaining, but they have reinforced since they came through Arkadelphia.[1]

On Monday last, the 18th, we had a fight at the Poison Springs on the Camden and Washington road, 15 miles from Camden. A forughing party variously estimated from 2 to 4 thousand we attacked at 12 Oclock by cannonading and then by small arms which lasted for three hours in the enemy was completed routed. Capturing 200 waggons and about 1250 mules and killed from 4 to 6 hundred and captured about 100 hundred prisoners. It was running fight. They were chased by the souldiers that we were with about three miles on foot and then the cavelory took them in hand and dont now know how far they pursued. I have said Fed yes of deepest dye negroes. I think there were 10 negroes killed to one white Fed. Just as I had said before, they made the negroes go in front and if the negro was wounded, our men would shoot him dead as they were passed and what negroes that were captured have, from the best information I can obtain, since been shot. I have seen enough myself to know it is correct our men is determine not to take negro prisoners, and if all of the negroes could have seen what occured that day, they would stay at home.

What I have seen reminds me of the talk I gave Henry and John. They may have been there as I have had no information as yet from home. If so, they are convinced by this time. (I cant believe that either went.) Among the killed was Dr. Rowlands Clabe and Kyles Berry and old man Edwards' boy was captured. I have told how they were disposed off.

From the best information, we lost about one hundred & sixty killed and wounded. A small portion killed; among them was George May, all the one that I knew.[2]

None of our company hurt its quite fortunate yet we were in the fight all the time and boys done well. Some few of them sick; none dangerous. None that we Know except Ed. Hicthcock, nothing cerious with him. We have been reinforced by infantry estimated at from 10 to 12 thousand. They are now in striking distance and there will be a move soon I predict to try Mr. Steel. Three days rations ordered to be cooked. This is done at the waggons and sent us. Would not be supprised we started by daylight in the morning. This I only have to judge from extreme circumstances, Although I am almost certain they will make no attack in Camden, owing to fortifications made by our own men last winter and faul. It is said to be well fortified and, of course, there will be no attack against works. Read this to Henry and John and it will remind them of what I told them.

This leaves me in fine health. Am quite anxious to hear from you, to learn all the news about Arkadelphia. Take it for granted...[portion illegible]...destroyed a great [?] of property as they had feather beds and all the comforts about ones house in their waggons. Clothing, etc. Now is the time...[page torn]...theives to in that country since both...[page torn]...miss are gone. I expect [steeling?]...[page torn]...on at a rapid rate. It is not...[page torn]...to tell you [portion illegible and page torn]...[V? C.?] would...[page torn]...it has been talk...[page torn]...for me it...[page torn]...since I left...[page torn].

The majority of the letters in the Spence Family Collection were written by Captain Alexander E. Spence of Company B, First Arkansas Infantry Regiment, or Captain Thomas F. Spence, Company E, Second Arkansas Mounted Rifles (Dismounted). This April 20, 1864, letter, however, clearly was written by neither of them, as Thomas Spence was killed December 31, 1862, in the Battle of Murfreesboro, Tennessee, and Alexander Spence and his unit were stationed in the mountains of northern Georgia when the Camden Expedition occurred. From the salutation and tone of the letter, it is obvious that the author was closely acquainted with Sallie Spence Hearn, to whom the letter is addressed.

While Sallie Hearn's younger brothers could not have been present at Poison Spring, her husband and an older brother

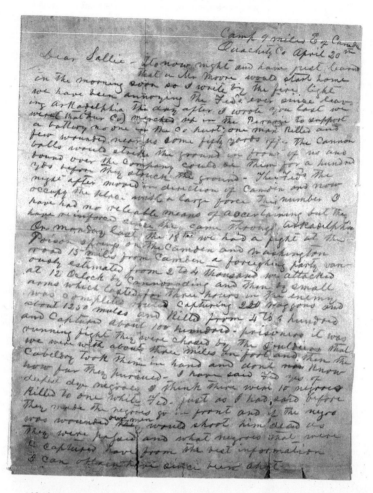

*Alfred Hearn wrote to his wife, Sallie Spence Hearn, about the Battle of Poison Spring: "What negroes that were captured have, from the best information I can obtain, since been shot. I have seen enough myself to know it is correct." (Courtesy of the Old State House Museum, Little Rock)*

were there and thus could have witnessed the actions described in the letter.[3] Dudley Spence, Sallie's brother, and her husband Alfred G. Hearn were serving in Captain Reuben C. Reed's Company of Robert C. Newton's Tenth Arkansas Cavalry.[4] Reed's company was raised relatively late in the war and Hearn and Spence would have been thirty-eight and forty-three years old respectively when they fought at Poison Spring. Their company was attached to Colonel W.H. Trader's Arkansas Cavalry Battalion at Poison Spring and had been part of the unit since at least November of 1863.[5]

Alfred Hearn, however, is almost certainly the author of this letter to "Dear Sallie."

The correspondent mentions "Henry and John" several times in the letter, and the context in which they are mentioned indicates that they were slaves of the writer. Alfred and Sallie Hearn owned male slaves aged thirty-three and seventeen in 1860, both of an age at which they could have fled Clark County to join the Union army by 1864.[6] Post-war records of the Freedmen's Bureau show that on January 1, 1866, John Hearn married Tempy Spence in a ceremony officiated by Justice of the Peace P.M. Carmichael. Freedmen's Bureau records also show that Solomon Spence, Sr. (Sallie Spence Hearn's father) had hired Tempy to work for him a week earlier for the sum of seven dollars per month and two suits of clothing.[7] It is likely that Tempy Spence was a former slave of Solomon Spence. If John Hearn was indeed a former slave of Alfred and Sallie Hearn, and Tempy Spence a slave of Solomon Spence, and if the two had adopted the names of their former masters, then they may well have known each other for some years and used their newfound freedom to marry and start a new life together. Thus, John Hearn could well be the John mentioned in the letter, and Alfred Hearn is the likely author.[8]

A final bit of evidence also favors Alfred Hearn as the author. At the request of the Old State House Museum, a forensics expert examined the Poison Spring letter and compared the handwriting on it with that of other authors represented in the Spence Family Collection. The closest thing to a handwriting match was contained in two letters written by Robert E. Hearn, a trooper in the Fourth Tennessee Cavalry, who incidentally never fought in the Trans-Mississippi. Robert Hearn was Alfred Hearn's brother, perhaps accounting for a similarity in their writing styles.

≈

1. The author is referring to the April 9-12 fighting at Prairie D'Ane near present-day Prescott in Nevada County, Arkansas.

2. George May was no stranger to the Spence family, having previously served with Tom Spence in Company E, Second Arkansas Mounted Rifles (Dismounted) before deserting and heading west to serve in Arkansas. Mark K. Christ, ed., *Getting Used to Being Shot At: The Spence Family Civil War Letters* (Fayetteville, Ark.: The University of Arkansas Press, 2002), 207.

3. Lieutenant R.C. Gilliam noted in a letter after the battle of Poison Spring that "Mr. Hearne is waiting." Ibid., 299. A postwar publication specifically stated that he was a veteran of Poison Spring. *Goodspeed Biographical and Historical Memoirs of Southern Arkansas* (Chicago: The Goodspeed Publishing Co., 1890), 173.

4. Unfortunately, the records of this regiment are not included in the National Archives' Compiled Service Records, though muster roles of Reed's company, including Dudley Spence and Alfred Hearn, were published after the war in Clark County newspapers. "Muster Roll of Rubin Reed's Company A (Tenth Regiment of Arkansas Cavalry)," *Clark County Historical Journal* (Winter, 1989-80), 181.

5. Lieutenant R.C. Gilliam noted the presence of Reed's outfit in a November 12, 1863, letter to his wife, writing: "We have preaching in camp three times on Sundays and prear [sic] meeting almost every night. Reed's company, form Clark [County], boast of having 5 or 7 I have forgotten which, preachers, Babtists [sic], Methodist and Presbyterians." James J. Hudson, ed., "From Paraclifta to Marks' Mill: The Civil War Correspondence of Lieutenant Robert C. Gilliam," *Arkansas Historical Quarterly* 17, no. 3 (Autumn, 1958), 281.

6. Population Schedule [Slave] of the Eighth Census of the United States, 1860, Arkansas, National Archives Microcopy No. 653, Roll 6.

7. Register of Contracts and Labor and Register of Marriages, 1865 to 1867, both in Field Office Records, Arkansas, Bureau of Refugees, Freedmen and Abandoned Lands, Record Group 105, National Archives.

8. Ibid.

# Poison Spring and Jenkins' Ferry: Racial Atrocities during the Camden Expedition *

## Gregory J. W. Urwin

At the outset of the Civil War, Camden, Arkansas, was a bustling commercial center on the Ouachita River roughly 120 miles south of Little Rock. Rows of trim white houses sheltered 2,219 people, making Camden the second largest city in the state.[1]

Yet when Major General Frederick Steele approached Camden with a Union army in April 1864, the place took on the appearance of a ghost town. Many of the city's young white males had gone off long ago to fight for Southern independence. The remaining white residents cowered in their homes, wondering what punishment the invaders might inflict on a community so firm in its support of the Confederacy. Such terror was a new experience for Camdenites, as no other large Union column had penetrated that far into southwestern Arkansas. As Private Wiley Britton of the Sixth Kansas Cavalry gloated: "Our rapid advance caused almost a complete panic among the rebel civilians,...so much so that they seemed to think the whole country was flooded with Yankees."[2]

That blue flood surged into Camden near dusk on April 15. "The awful day of all days—the dread event feared for years,"

---

* This article is a revised version of "'Cut to Pieces and Gone to Hell': The Poison Spring Massacre," which appeared in *North & South* 3 (August 2000): 45-57.

local merchant John W. Brown scribbled in his diary. "About 6 O' clock, an enemy infuriated by combat & hunger came rushing down our main street and diverging into the cross streets.... Northern muskets, swords & bayonets glittering with the last rays of the setting sun with fierce imprecations and hideous shouts of exultation."[3]

Steele, the commander of the Union Department of Arkansas and VII Army Corps, drew his army from two sources. Nine thousand men grouped in one infantry division and one cavalry division accompanied Steele when he left Little Rock on March 23, 1864. A second column under Brigadier General John M. Thayer had already marched from Fort Smith two days earlier with the Frontier Division. It contained just under five thousand troops in two infantry brigades and one of cavalry. The two Federal columns rendezvoused on the Little Missouri River south of Arkadelphia on April 9.[4]

Thayer's Second Brigade included the First and Second Kansas Colored Infantry, the first black regiments ever committed to an active combat role in a major Union offensive in Arkansas. That fact infuriated Confederate soldiers and civilians alike. "Only one thing stirred my Southern blood to heat," admitted a Camden housewife, "was when a negro regiment passed my home going to fight our own dear men."[5]

Steele's ultimate destination was Shreveport, Louisiana, on the Red River, where he planned to join a larger Union army and a gunboat flotilla under Major General Nathaniel P. Banks. Banks wanted Steele to assist in an invasion of Texas and the seizure of vast supplies of cotton for profit-hungry Northern speculators.[6]

Steele's route south was not an easy one. Lieutenant General Edmund Kirby Smith, the commander of the Confederacy's Trans-Mississippi Department, concentrated much of his strength in Louisiana to oppose Banks, but he left six thousand cavalry behind to defend southern Arkansas. Most of these Rebel troopers were well-mounted and armed with long-range Enfield and Richmond rifle muskets, which enabled them to function as potent mounted infantry. Beginning on April 2, the Confederates subjected Steele's main column to constant harassment, contesting river crossings and pressing his rear guard. "I don't think there was a day passed without some one being Shot," claimed one Union infantryman. The Confederates continued their hit-and-run tactics even after Steele and Thayer united on the Little Missouri.[7]

Though Steele's soldiers cursed enemy bushwhacking and muddy roads, the most formidable adversary they encountered was hunger. The Federals passed through a country that had been scoured by Confederate foragers since the fall of 1863. By the time the invaders reached Camden, they had been on half-rations for three weeks, and they immediately searched the city for anything to eat. "The soldiers dashed to our doors demanding food," John Brown confided to his diary. "I soon handed out all the victuals which were on hand, cooked. After dark they brook into the smoke house & commenced carrying off as they wanted." Mrs. A.J. Marshall, a schoolteacher, watched in horror as blue foot soldiers "broke open the smokehouse with one blow of the butt-end of their muskets, stuck their bayonets through as many joints of meat as would stick on them, filled seives and boxes with meat, rice, sugar, coffee, flour, etc."[8]

While the larders of Camden afforded temporary relief to the famished Union troops, Steele faced another problem. His future mobility depended on providing sufficient forage for the twelve thousand horses and mules attached to his army. As Captain Charles A. Henry, Steele's chief quartermaster, commented, "The difficulty of procuring forage occasioned great uneasiness, as we were without any base of supplies and with an active enemy in front."[9]

Fortunately, Captain Henry learned that five thousand bushels of corn had been stored at some farms sixteen miles

west of Camden. He quickly assembled a forage train of 198
wagons to collect this prize, which could be converted into meal
for Steele's soldiers or feed for his livestock. With thousands of
enemy cavalry lurking in the vicinity, Steele called on the
Frontier Division to furnish a train escort. General Thayer
assigned more than six hundred infantry and cavalry to that
duty—438 officers and men from the First Kansas Colored
Infantry and 197 troopers in detachments taken from the
Second, Sixth, and Fourteenth Kansas Cavalry. Thayer also sent
along thirty-three artillerymen and two ten-pound James rifles
in Lieutenant William W. Haines's section of the Second
Independent Battery, Indiana Light Artillery. To command the
train and escort, Thayer chose James M. Williams, the idealis-
tic colonel of the First Kansas Colored. A former lawyer,
Williams was noted for his zeal, energy, and efficiency, and had
led his regiment to victory in some hotly contested actions in
Indian Territory.[10]

Colonel Williams roused his column early on Sunday, April
17, and conducted it west along the Camden-Washington Road.
The Federals marched eighteen miles and went into camp along
White Oak Creek, where Williams dispatched details to seize any
corn found at farms and plantations within a six-mile radius.
Correctly divining Williams's mission, Confederate patrols
reached several of these places first and burned approximately
twenty-five hundred bushels. The Federals loaded what remained
aboard 141 wagons and reassembled at their camp by midnight.[11]

Williams commenced his homeward march at the crack of
dawn on April 18. As the column plodded toward a rising sun,
the conscientious colonel split off foraging details to fill his
empty wagons from farms along his route. "There being but
few wagon loads of corn to be found at any one place," Williams
explained, "I was obliged to detach portions of the command in
different directions to load the wagons until nearly my whole
available force was so employed." These side trips and the extra

labor weighed heavily on the footsore First Kansas Colored Infantry, which had received only fifteen hours of rest during the past seventy-eight. By mid-morning, one hundred black soldiers were so exhausted that their officers considered them unfit for duty.[12]

Williams proceeded four toilsome miles to a point known as "Cross-Roads," where a welcome sight greeted his eyes. Following the departure of the forage train the previous day, General Thayer organized a 501-man relief column under Captain William M. Duncan to cover Williams's return. Duncan had covered twelve miles before dark on the seventeenth, which allowed him to effect a quick junction with Williams the next morning. The relief force included 383 officers and men from Duncan's own regiment, the Eighteenth Iowa Infantry, ninety-three horsemen from the Second, Sixth, and Fourteenth Kansas Cavalry, and a section of two twelve-pound mountain howitzers manned by one officer and twenty-four troopers detached from the Sixth Kansas Cavalry. Duncan's arrival gave Williams a total force of 1,169, but many of his cavalrymen would deliberately lag behind to loot nearby farms.[13]

Keeping the original train escort and Duncan's contingent separate, Williams had the newcomers fall in at the rear of the column. The Federals proceeded eastward, approaching an area that the locals called Poison Spring. A mile down the road, the cavalry screening Williams's advance spotted a number of mounted Confederate pickets. This by itself was no cause for alarm. Duncan's cavalry had skirmished with enemy patrols throughout its outward march the previous day. Williams's advance guard spurred forward and the pickets gave ground as expected. A mile closer to Camden, however, the Yankees topped a hill beside the road around ten in the morning and sighted a sizeable Rebel skirmish line bearing down on them. If Colonel Williams intended to bring corn to Camden, he would have to fight a battle at Poison Spring.[14]

Those oncoming skirmishers represented the lead elements of 3,621 Confederate cavalry and horse artillery who were converging on Poison Spring as quick as their mounts could carry them. The officer responsible for this timely concentration was Brigadier General John S. Marmaduke, a combative West Point graduate who commanded a Missouri cavalry division with headquarters at Woodlawn, fourteen miles southwest of Camden. On the morning of April 17, Marmaduke's scouts brought him word of Williams's foraging expedition. Marmaduke wanted to attack, but he had only 486 troops on hand in Colonel Colton Greene's understrength brigade and Captain S.S. Harris's four-gun battery. Marmaduke immediately requested aid from Brigadier General James F. Fagan, the commander of an Arkansas cavalry division. Fagan generously loaned him Brigadier General William L. Cabell's twelve-hundred-man brigade, Colonel William A. Crawford's three-hundred-man brigade, and the four guns of Captain W. M. Hughey's battery. For some undisclosed reason, Fagan chose not to accompany these units himself and command of them reverted to Cabell.[15]

Setting out at sunset to intercept Williams, Marmaduke rode two miles until he met some excited scouts. They announced that the Federals had been reinforced and now numbered twenty-five hundred men. Discouraged by the grossly exaggerated estimate, Marmaduke returned to Woodlawn, but he was not willing to let Williams escape.[16]

At eleven that night, Marmaduke began writing a dispatch intended for Major General Sterling Price, a fellow Missourian who headed the Confederate District of Arkansas. Marmaduke proposed to set out the next day with Cabell, Crawford, and Greene to block the Camden-Washington Road near Poison Spring. He asked that any additional troops Price could scrape together join him there by eight a.m.[17]

Price liked Marmaduke's show of initiative, and he just happened to have another cavalry force bivouacked at Woodlawn.

Brigadier General Samuel B. Maxey's 1,335-man division had recently transferred from Indian Territory. Maxey's toughest brigade consisted of 625 Texans under Colonel Charles DeMorse. DeMorse also enjoyed the services of Captain W. Butler Krumbhaar's Texas Battery, with its thirty artillerists and four guns. By far the most exotic component in the division was Colonel Tandy Walker's Second Indian Brigade, two Choctaw regiments totaling 680 men. With their war paint, ragged clothing, and hats sporting peacock feathers and other plumage, the Choctaws looked fierce, but their military effectiveness was questionable. Many of Walker's troops were white men who had joined Indian regiments because discipline in such outfits tended to be lax.[18]

*Colonel Tandy Walker's First Choctaw Regiment was blamed for much of the butchery that followed the battle of Poison Spring, with one white Confederate soldier writing, "over a small portion of the field we saw at least 40 bodies lying in all conceivable attitudes, some scalped & nearly all stripped by the bloodthirsty Choctaws." (Courtesy of the Oklahoma Historical Society)*

On the morning of April 18, Price directed Maxey to take his division at once to Lee's plantation near Poison Spring and join forces with Marmaduke. With DeMorse's Texans in the lead, Maxey moved out at seven o'clock. Price also sent his personal escort, the three hundred troopers of Major Robert C. Wood's Fourteenth Missouri Battalion, to assist Marmaduke.[19]

The eager Marmaduke was in the saddle that morning well before Maxey or Wood. He had his Missourians and Cabell's

Arkansans in motion by sunrise, and he reached the Poison Spring area first. Probing west along the Camden-Washington Road, he encountered the Union advance at ten o'clock. As the general's escort drove the Federals from a hill on the south side of the road, Marmaduke had Cabell dismount most of his men and bring them up to join Hughey's Arkansas Battery in holding the high ground. The Arkansans formed astride the road, with Crawford's brigade to the right, Cabell's brigade to the left, and skirmishers out in front. Cabell placed a mounted battalion on each flank of this line. Marmaduke bolstered the Arkansans' position by unlimbering Harris's Missouri Battery to Crawford's right, but he kept Greene back for the time being as a mounted reserve. A little later, he positioned the Fourteenth Missouri Battalion to Crawford's right. As an added precaution, Cabell sent the Second Arkansas Cavalry clattering two miles to the rear in case any Federals in Camden tried to come to Williams's assistance.[20]

The head of Maxey's division reached the scene just as the Arkansans finished deploying. Aware that Maxey was his senior in rank, Marmaduke reported to him for orders. To his credit, Maxey declined, saying that the Missourian had set the trap and should direct the fight.[21]

A grateful Marmaduke sketched a simple battle plan. He suggested that Maxey's men dismount and attack the Federals from the south. Once Maxey was warmly engaged and the enemy's attention turned in his direction, Hughey and Harris would open fire with their eight guns and the two Arkansas brigades would sweep in the from the east. Greene's brigade would stand by and support either Maxey or Cabell as circumstances dictated.[22]

When Marmaduke revealed his presence at Poison Spring, Colonel Williams responded by rushing the original Union escort to the front of the forage train. He arrayed these troops in a battle line facing east—Haines's two James rifles on the road, five companies of the First Kansas Colored on either side of the artillery, and cavalry on the flanks. Captain Duncan had his contingent adopt a similar formation behind the train. Hoping to bait the Rebels into showing their full power, Williams ordered Haines to throw a few shells in Marmaduke's direction, but this challenge elicited only scattered small arms fire from Cabell's skirmishers.[23]

Soon, however, Williams and his officers became aware of more Confederates approaching from the south. Maxey's division was advancing toward the Federal right flank with DeMorse's Texans on the right and Walker's Choctaws on the left. Timber, underbrush, and ravines obscured Maxey's numbers, but these same features impeded his progress. "I found great difficulty in preserving alignment and connection," complained Colonel DeMorse. Krumbhaar's Texas Battery, which brought along no axes, had to call for help in getting its guns through a patch of saplings.[24]

The discovery of this new threat necessitated a hasty redeployment of Union forces. Williams began by sending about a hundred troopers from the Second and Sixth Kansas Cavalry to test Maxey's strength. As the cavalry rode off, Major Richard G. Ward, the First Kansas Colored's acting commander, arranged his regiment in an L-shaped line. He left Companies C, I, D, and F and one James rifle facing east, positioned Companies A, B, E, and H south of the Camden-Washington Road to counter Maxey, and placed Companies G and K in reserve. Haines's second gun supported Ward's southward-facing right wing. Warned by Williams "to keep a sharp lookout for a movement upon his rear and right flank," Captain Duncan wheeled the Eighteenth Iowa, his mountain howitzers, and his cavalry to the right to meet the Choctaws composing Maxey's left wing.[25]

Williams's mounted reconnaissance force rode four hundred yards before it made contact with Maxey's labored advance. As the Kansans urged their steeds across an open field, the bushes in front of them suddenly blossomed with the fire and smoke of exploding musketry. Dismounted skirmishers from DeMorse's Twenty-ninth Texas Cavalry hit one Union lieutenant and possibly emptied a few other saddles. The shaken Federals broke to the rear, carrying away the stricken officer. The blue cavalrymen finally rallied on Major Ward's right wing, and he posted them to his right to fill the gap between the First Kansas Colored and Duncan's command.[26]

No sooner had Ward completed these dispositions than he and his black soldiers became the targets of a vicious crossfire. One thousand yards to the east, the guns of Hughey and Harris spewed a barrage of shot and shell aimed at suppressing Federal efforts to resist Maxey. Ensconced on a knoll six to seven hundred yards from the First Kansas Colored, Krumbhaar's four guns added their booming voices to the din. Lieutenant William M. Stafford, Krumbhaar's second in command, pulled out his watch to note the time. It was noon. The Battle of Poison Spring had begun.[27]

The three Rebel batteries concentrated their fire on the center of the First Kansas Colored's line. Colonel Williams characterized the cannonade as "incessant and well-directed," but the former slaves he had trained as soldiers endured their trial with quiet fortitude. "Although this was much the severest artillery fire that any of the men had ever before been subjected to," Major Ward pointed out, even the greenest recruits "were as cool as veterans and patiently awaited the onset of the enemy." Williams estimated the number of Rebel guns at nine, which told him he was outnumbered. Nevertheless, he resolved to hold his ground as long as possible, certain that General Steele would hear the roar of battle and come racing to the rescue. It was a misplaced hope.[28]

After about thirty minutes, the Confederate artillery slackened its fire as DeMorse's brigade neared the First Kansas Colored's right wing. The broken nature of the ground between

DeMorse and the black Federals made long-range shooting a waste of ammunition, but Colonel Williams was undismayed. He allowed the Texans to close to one hundred yards and then had the First Kansas Colored unleash a fusillade of "buck and ball." The Texans raised their rifles in reply, punctuating their shots with shrill Rebel yells. For fifteen minutes, the opposing lines blazed away at each other. Many of DeMorse's men took aim at the crew of the James rifle to their front. Major Ward later reported that the Texans "disabled more than half of the gunners" during this phase of the battle.[29]

The First Kansas Colored was renowned for fast and deadly shooting, however, and its stinging mixture of bullets and buckshot proved too much for DeMorse's brigade. Lieutenant Stafford, who had helped move Krumbhaar's Texas Battery to within three hundred yards of the First Kansas, recalled that "the engagement was brisk, to use the mildest term—the fire was extraordinarily heavy, and we began to believe the force against which we were contending was decidedly heavier than was reported." General Marmaduke and other Confederate officers present would claim that they encountered two black regiments at Poison Spring instead of one—an unintended tribute to the fighting prowess of the First Kansas Colored.[30]

An abrupt panic seized DeMorse's left and center, and those troops fled to the rear. Cool and quick in a crisis, Captain Krumbhaar immediately instructed his gunners to load with shell and cut their fuses to explode at two seconds. Then he gave the command to fire by half battery. Two guns at a time, Krumbhaar's artillerists hammered the First Kansas Colored with devastatingly accurate salvoes. Seeing DeMorse's troopers recoil, the Arkansas and Missouri batteries "again opened their infernal cross-fires," as Major Ward put it. DeMorse's men observed the effects of this shelling, and they soon heeded the rallying cries shouted by their brigade commander and his assistant adjutant general, Captain M.L. Bell.[31]

While the First Kansas Colored mauled DeMorse's Texans, Tandy Walker's Choctaws kept a respectful distance from the Eighteenth Iowa Infantry, which Captain Duncan had posted behind a thickly wooded ravine. The Indians hesitated to get entangled in that natural obstacle and turn themselves into easy targets for the Iowans. Colonel Walker offered a lame excuse for his inaction. He reported that some Union cavalry had gained his left flank, but the truth was that the Choctaws' line overlapped Duncan's. Despite Walker's passivity, Duncan declined a request from Colonel Williams to send four infantry companies to reinforce the First Kansas. The captain replied that he was hard pressed and had no men to spare.[32]

Peering through the smoke produced by exploding artillery shells, Major Ward spotted DeMorse's brigade reforming for a second assault. In response to Ward's plea for more troops, Colonel Williams released Companies G and K from reserve to bolster the First Kansas Colored's right wing. Ward incorporated these two companies into his southward-facing line just in time to meet DeMorse's next onslaught. The Texans returned to the fight in two columns, and Ward could hear them "yelling like fiends" to keep up their courage. Colonel Williams observed that the enemy's "continuous cheering" was so loud "so as to drown out even the roar of the musketry." Instead of ceasing fire, the three Confederate batteries slightly increased their elevation, hurling their shells over their own troops to burst above the First Kansas Colored.[33]

Colonel Williams sat calmly on his horse amid the whirr of shrapnel, permitting the Texans to come well within one hundred yards before he shouted to Ward's reinforced line to open fire. Once again, the blacks subjected their assailants to repeated doses of buck and ball. The Texans plunged into that leaden storm, determined to drive their attack home. "The noise and din of...this almost hand-to-hand conflict was the loudest and most terrific it has been my lot to listen to,"

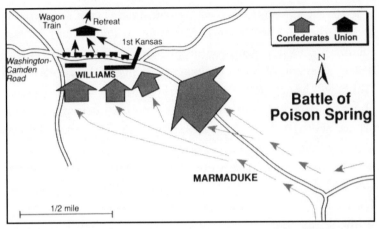

*Battle of Poison Spring. Map by Steve Scallion. (Courtesy of the Arkansas Historic Preservation Program)*

Williams recalled. Twice the Union commander saw a Rebel battle flag fall from the hands of a wounded color bearer, but each time some brave soul sprang forward to raise it again.[34]

Several minutes into this ferocious musketry duel, one of DeMorse's regiments, the Twenty-ninth Texas Cavalry, edged close enough to Ward's position to recognize the opposing regiment. A wave of redoubled fury swept the Texan ranks, and the men announced their identity by shrieking: "You First Kansas Niggers now buck to the Twenty-ninth Texas!" These two units had met earlier at the Battle of Honey Springs in Indian Territory on July 17, 1863. In a fair, stand-up fight, the First Kansas outshot the Twenty-ninth Texas, forcing the shaken Confederates to withdraw without their colors. Ashamed at having been bested by former slaves, the Texans burned for revenge.[35]

As in the first attack, the Rebels concentrated much of their fire on the James rifle from the Second Indiana Light Battery attached to Major Ward's right wing. Eventually, all but two of the ten-pounder's crew had been hit or were hugging cover. When Ward pointed that out to Colonel Williams, the latter ordered the endangered piece to the rear. The Confederates noticed the blue artillerymen preparing to limber, and a gray column bounded forward to prevent the gun's escape. Only the steady bravery of one Indiana cannoneer, Private Alonso Hinshaw, cheated the Rebels of their prize. Working alone, Hinshaw loaded his gun with double-canister, inserted a friction primer, jerked the lanyard, and sprayed the oncoming Texans with a withering cone of cast-iron balls, causing them to scatter.[36]

Hinshaw's parting shot knocked the wind out of DeMorse's attack. Fifteen minutes of unrelenting punishment told the Texans that they could not budge Ward's quick-shooting blacks. Without abandoning their formations, the Rebels sullenly backed away, and their weary adversaries soon stopped firing.[37]

The First Kansas Colored had prevailed a second time, but victory against such odds carried a high price. To Colonel Williams, it looked like half of the men in Ward's right wing were dead or wounded, and three of those six companies had lost all their officers. The black soldiers had also depleted their ammunition, and they searched the cartridge boxes of slain comrades for a few more rounds. Over on the left wing, the Second Indiana's other gun had expended all its projectiles except solid shot, which was of limited use against enemy personnel—especially at close range. Williams directed Lieutenant Haines to retire both of his James rifles and report to Captain Duncan at the rear of the train.[38]

As Williams fretted over the weakened state of the First Kansas Colored, the Confederates brought up reinforcements for a third attack. Two sharp repulses had shown General Maxey that he required more weight to make any headway against such stubborn opposition. He was also tired of not receiving stronger support from the other friendly units on the field. Asserting his status as senior Confederate commander, Maxey summoned Greene's Missouri brigade to fall in on DeMorse's right and strike the First Kansas Colored's center during the next advance.[39]

Watching the approach of Greene's Missourians, Colonel Williams knew that the First Kansas Colored was in no shape to beat off another heavy thrust. He shouted to Major Ward to hold the First Kansas in place while he rode to the rear to redeploy the Eighteenth Iowa to cover the black regiment's retreat. Just as Williams applied spurs to his horse, a Confederate bullet slammed into the animal, and it crumpled to the ground. Major Ward offered the colonel his own mount, and Williams galloped off on his urgent errand. Before Williams could reposition the Eighteenth Iowa, however, a massive gray wave swamped the decimated First Kansas Colored.[40]

The third Confederate attack at Poison Spring was a model of tactical coordination. First, DeMorse's Texans tramped forward to trade volleys with Ward's right wing. Minutes later, Greene's Missourians threw themselves at the Federals. "The left and center were hotly pressed," Greene commented, "when I advanced at the double-quick with loud cheers, passed the line, delivered several well-directed volleys, and charged the enemy through burning woods and dense smoke." A grateful Colonel DeMorse testified that the Missourians joined the fight "in the very moment when most effective." With DeMorse and Greene warmly engaged, Maxey sent word to General Cabell to drive west along the Camden-Washington Road with his Arkansas division. As Maxey's battle plan came together, he noted happily: "The whole line moved forward like a sheet of living fire carrying death and destruction before it."[41]

The First Kansas Colored had no hope of withstanding the combined power of four brigades. The first elements of the regiment to give way were the two leftmost companies, C and I, stationed north of the Camden–Washington Road. Lieutenant William C. Gibbons, Ward's adjutant, sensed these companies were about to be outflanked by Cabell's Arkansans and pulled them back to the head of the forage train. This move exposed the rest of the First Kansas Colored's left flank even as the reg-

iment sustained increasing pressure all along its front. Major
Ward ordered the eight companies still under his control to
retire on the train. At the same time, he changed front to the
left to refuse his vulnerable flank.[42]

Ward tried to make a stand in front of the train, but the
momentum had shifted to the Confederates. DeMorse's Texans
pounced on Ward's right flank and raked the First Kansas with
a telling enfilade fire. The Rebels drove the Federals through the
train with heavy loss. As they swirled around clumps of fallen
blacks, some Arkansans paused to see if any were still breathing.
"If the negro was wounded," recounted one of Cabell's troopers,
"our men would shoot him dead as they were passed."
Lieutenant Stafford of Krumbhaar's battery witnessed the same
behavior among DeMorse's Texans. "No black prisoners were
taken," he recorded in his journal. One wounded African-
American refused to die meekly and sank his teeth into a Rebel's
calf until someone crushed his skull with a rifle butt. Catching
glimpses of these atrocities, uninjured First Kansas personnel
began leaving the firing line to help wounded comrades to the
rear, which undercut Major Ward's efforts to maintain resistance. Other black soldiers lost their nerve entirely and bolted.[43]

At length, Ward bade the First Kansas to quit the train and
regroup behind Captain Duncan's Eighteenth Iowa Infantry,
which had taken shelter among the buildings and fences of Lee's
plantation. Williams, Ward, and other First Kansas officers
rallied a portion of their men and formed a ragged line on the
Eighteenth Iowa's left, but nothing could stem the Rebel tide.
Bellowing "Here's your mule!" and raising cheers for Missouri,
Greene's brigade bulled forward and evicted the Federals from
the plantation grounds. The Iowans reformed in the thick brush
beyond the Lee place, but the Missourians charged and blud-
geoned them back again. This scene repeated itself five more
times as the Eighteenth Iowa would retreat a short distance and
then turn around to pepper the Confederates with musketry. In

this way, Duncan delayed his opponents for more than an hour, the Iowans emptying their cartridge boxes in the process. The Eighteenth Iowa might have been cut off and annihilated had Tandy Walker kept a tighter rein on his Choctaws. Rather than pursue the beaten Federals, the Indians raced toward the abandoned forage wagons in a mad scramble for food and plunder.[44]

While the Eighteenth Iowa bought valuable time, Colonel Williams shepherded the broken remnants of his command north toward the refuge of a swamp. Williams's escape route led over steep hills and deep ravines covered with timber. The ground was impassable for the Union artillery, which was spiked and left behind. At Williams's behest, Lieutenant Richard L. Phillips of the Sixth Kansas Cavalry threw some skittish Union horsemen into line in a feeble attempt to shield wounded black stragglers. "My men," Phillips insisted, "acted as well as men could act under the circumstances; for the enemy were following the negroes and pouring a heavy fire into their ranks." Riding up a hill past the spot where the Second Indiana Light Battery abandoned its James rifles, Lieutenant Gibbons turned to "distinctly see the rebels shooting our brave but fatigued boys."[45]

Despite the Eighteenth Iowa's valiant exertions, the Confederates chased the retreating Federals for two and a half miles. The whole Union escort might have been killed or captured had not General Maxey called a halt to the pursuit in the late afternoon. Maxey was aware that the sounds of the battle could be heard at Camden. He did not want any enemy relief column to plow into him from behind while his troops were scattered. He therefore instructed his subordinates to reassemble their units and remove their captures to a place of safety. Unimpeded by the Rebels, Williams and his surviving troops traced a circuitous route back to Camden. The swiftest of these fugitives reached friendly lines around eight o'clock that evening.[46]

Maxey's precautions were commendable but unnecessary. The first rumble of artillery fire from Poison Spring prompted General Thayer to call out what remained of the Frontier Division's cavalry at Camden and have the men saddle their horses. Although General Steele could hear the firing as well, he issued no orders to organize a relief column, much to the bafflement of his officers. From Fort Smith, the home base of the Frontier Division, the disgusted editor of a Unionist newspaper would charge, "We have it from reliable sources that Gen. Thayer repeatedly asked permission to sally out with his Division to cover the retreat of the devoted little band, but of no avail."[47]

Back at the wagon train, the Rebels celebrated their triumph with an orgy of barbarism. A black soldier feigning death listened in silent horror while execution squads from the Twenty-ninth Texas Cavalry roamed the battlefield to finish off the First Kansas Colored's wounded. As the Texans proceeded with their bloody work, they chanted a ghastly litany. "Where is the First Kansas Nigger now?" some would hoot. "All cut to pieces and gone to hell by bad management," others would answer. Colonel DeMorse did not acknowledge a massacre, but he boasted in his official report: "But few prisoners were brought in by my men." Detailed to drive away the captured wagons, troopers from Cabell's division played a sickening game with their fallen enemies. Each Arkansan vied to see if he could crush the most "nigger heads" under his wagon wheels.[48]

An Arkansas trooper who identified himself simply as "B" described the battlefield in a letter to the *Washington (Ark.) Telegraph*. It is clear that he and his comrades regarded the dead black soldiers as only so much destroyed property: "We rode over the field after the fight, and when we beheld so many stalwart negroes weltering in their gore, we could not suppress a sigh over their hard fate—the poor dupes of a miserable set of fanatics and demagogues. Would it not have been better, could we have captured these able-bodied men, to have taken them back to the interior and put them to hard work—light work compared to the burthens of their present taskmasters?"[49]

The Choctaw brigade, which had shown little stomach for combat that day, outdid all other Confederate units in the post-battle butchery. "The havoc among the negroes had been tremendous," wrote Lieutenant Stafford, "over a small portion of the field we saw at least 40 dead bodies lying in all conceivable attitudes, some scalped & nearly all stripped by the blood-thirsty Choctaws." "You ought to see Indians fight Negroes," exclaimed Private Charles T. Anderson of the Second Arkansas Cavalry, "kill and scalp them. Let me tell you, I never expected to see as many dead Negroes again. They were so thick you could walk on them."[50]

The Choctaws' rage did not abate after the African-Americans were dead. In addition to scalping and stripping, the Indians devised novel ways to desecrate black corpses. The *Washington Telegraph*, the nearest Confederate newspaper to the scene of slaughter, gleefully reported the following example of what the newspaper referred to as "Choctaw Humor": "After the battle of Poison Springs, the Choctaws buried a Yankee in an ordinary grave. For a headstone they put up a stiff negro buried to the waist. For a footstone another negro reversed out from the waist to the heels."[51]

The Poison Spring Massacre has gone down in history as the worst war crime ever committed on Arkansas soil. It exemplified the Confederate reaction to the Union Army's increasing reliance on black soldiers. As products of a slave culture, most white Southerners grew up believing that African-Americans were inherently savage and had to be kept in bondage to lead orderly and productive lives. Remove their shackles, and blacks would revert into murderous beasts intent on slaying all whites regardless of sex or age. It was this largely baseless fear that caused Southerners to react so wildly whenever the North's abolitionist minority condemned their social system. Upon Abraham Lincoln's 1860 election as president on a platform pledged to the containment and eventual elimination of slavery, the persisting dread of servile insurrection stampeded the Deep South into dissolving the Union and seeking independence.[52]

Steeped in such values, Confederates could not help but regard Lincoln's Emancipation Proclamation and his recruitment of black soldiers as the ultimate war crime—the inauguration of a merciless race war dedicated not merely to the destruction of the Southern way of life, but to the extermination of the South's white population. Since Little Rock's occupation by Federal forces in September 1863, the *Washington Telegraph* had functioned as the voice of Confederate Arkansas. Its editor, John R. Eakin, compared the "crime of Lincoln in seducing our slaves into the ranks of his army" to "those stupendous wrongs against humanity, shocking to the moral sense of the world, like Herod's massacre of the Innocents, or the eve of St. Bartholomew." Because the Federals had violated the rules of civilized warfare by giving blacks weapons, Eakin argued, incidents like the Poison Spring Massacre were perfectly justified. "It follows irresistibly," he declared, "that we *cannot* treat negroes taken in arms as prisoners of war, without a destruction of the social system for which we contend." In other words, it was better to kill rebellious slaves, whether they wore Union uniforms or not, to prevent other bondsmen from following their example. One of Cabell's Arkansans expressed this mind set in a letter to his wife: "Our men are determined not to take negro prisoners and if all the negroes could have seen what occurred today, they would stay at home." These were the same sentiments that inspired Major General Nathan Bedford Forrest's Confederate soldiers as they cut down black prisoners taken at Fort Pillow, Tennessee, six days before Poison Spring.[53]

Defeat at Poison Spring cost the Union Army 301 killed, wounded, and missing. More than half of these losses belonged to the First Kansas Colored Infantry, which suffered 117 killed, but carried off 65 of its wounded. General Marmaduke reported that 125 white Federals were taken prisoner. The Confederates also captured four guns and 198 wagons, but 30 of the latter had to be burned because not enough draft animals were left alive to pull them off the battlefield. For Frederick Steele's army at Camden, the loss of the forage train meant prolonged hunger. The setback also underlined the danger of operating so deep in hostile territory without sufficient logistical support. Confederate casualty reports were incomplete, but Maxey estimated his total losses at fewer than 145.[54]

The Federal forces caught at Poison Spring operated under debilitating handicaps. In addition to being outnumbered by a wide margin, Colonel Williams did not have enough time to organize his original escort and Captain Duncan's relief column into a cohesive team. Early in the battle, well before the Eighteenth Iowa Infantry faced any significant pressure, Duncan curtly refused a request from Williams to move four companies to the head of the train to reinforce the First Kansas Colored. The Iowans subsequently redeemed themselves with their tenacious rear-guard performance in covering Williams's retreat, but the same cannot be said of the Union cavalry. Wherever the action heated up, the blue troopers would drift away from the firing line. By the time of the third Confederate assault, which cracked the First Kansas Colored, the cavalry units deployed between the black regiment and the Eighteenth Iowa seem to have abandoned their posts completely, presenting DeMorse's Texans with an easy opportunity to enfilade Major Ward's right flank.[55]

Although not every component in Colonel Williams's escort fought with the same spirit as the First Kansas Colored, the blame for the Poison Spring disaster belonged primarily to General Steele. The Union commander displayed sheer recklessness in sending such a vulnerable detachment so far from his

*Colonel Samuel J. Crawford led the Second Kansas Colored Infantry. His regiment avenged the Poison Spring massacre by killing Confederate prisoners and wounded at Jenkins' Ferry. (Courtesy of the Gregory J.W. Urwin Collection)*

main body, especially since he knew he faced an aggressive and highly mobile foe.[56] On the Confederate side, General Marmaduke deserves high marks for mobilizing a force large enough to exploit Steele's mistake, but he failed to handle his brigades properly once battle was joined. Victory hung in the balance until General Maxey took charge and coordinated the final Rebel assault.

The main legacy of Poison Spring was the addition of an ugly dimension to the Civil War in Arkansas. In keeping with the prevailing racial prejudices of the day, many of Steele's white soldiers exhibited a callous disregard for the murder of their black comrades. Others were outraged by the atrocities at Poison Spring. "I want no [Confederate] prisoners," stormed Corporal Charles O. Musser of the Twenty-ninth Iowa Infantry. "If they [the Confederates] raise the Black flag, we can fight under it.... I say give the rebbels no quarter, and the feeling is the same throughout the army in the west. *We will retaliate.*"[57]

If there was one Union unit at Camden that subscribed unanimously to these sentiments, it had to be Steele's other black regiment, the Second Kansas Colored Infantry. On the evening of April 19, Colonel Samuel J. Crawford, the Second's no-nonsense commander, summoned his officers to a meeting to discuss the Poison Spring Massacre. With cold-blooded deliberateness, that assemblage solemnly swore that "the regiment would take no prisoners so long as the Rebels continued to murder our men." The Second Kansas Colored soon found an opportunity to redeem that merciless pledge.[58]

Shortly after General Steele captured Camden, his intelligence sources began advising him that General Banks had been defeated on the Red River and was in full retreat. Two couriers from Banks, who reached Steele on April 18 and 22, respectively, confirmed these disturbing reports. Steele received another blow on the twenty-second when he learned that Lieutenant General Edmund Kirby Smith, the commander of the Confederacy's Trans-Mississippi Department, had arrived near Camden with eight thousand infantry. These three divisions were fresh from their recent victory in Louisiana and spoiling for a fight. That same day, Brigadier General James F. Fagan organized four thousand Rebel horsemen into a strike force to cut Steele's communications between Camden and the Arkansas River. Fagan drew blood on April 25 at Marks' Mills, where he captured a 240-wagon Union train and annihilated the reinforced brigade that Steele had detailed to escort it to Pine Bluff. Rather than let his army be trapped south of the Ouachita River, Steele quietly evacuated Camden on the evening of April 26 and headed back to Little Rock.[59]

Kirby Smith overtook the fleeing Federals on April 30 at Jenkins' Ferry after they got bogged down in the flooded bottoms fringing the south side of the Saline River. While Steele's cavalry, artillery, and other impedimenta sloshed through two muddy miles to cross a hastily constructed pontoon bridge, his infantry turned around to hold Kirby Smith at bay. The Second Kansas Colored gladly took its place in the battle line, and as an Arkansas brigade came within range, Colonel Crawford shouted to his 660 black soldiers, "Aim low, and give them hell."[60]

Well into the battle, a section from Captain Samuel T. Ruffner's Missouri Battery unlimbered a pair of field pieces opposite the Second Kansas Colored. Crawford was not the kind of officer to sit still and watch his regiment get pounded to bits. Instead, he ordered a charge. Closely supported by the Twenty-ninth Iowa Infantry, the Second Kansas Colored immobilized the enemy guns with a volley that killed most of their battery horses. A second volley scattered the section's infantry supports. Then the Second Kansas leveled its bayonets and raced forward, the men shouting, "Poison Springs!" The blacks overran their objective in a matter of seconds, plunging their bayonets into every Confederate they could catch, including three artillerists who tried to surrender.[61]

Sweeping into the battery position hard on the heels of the Second Kansas, the Twenty-ninth Iowa Infantry beheld some grisly incidents. As Private Milton P. Chambers of the Twenty-ninth revealed: "One of our boys seen a little negro pounding a wounded reb in the head with the but of his gun and asked him what he was doing. The negro replied he is not dead yet!" Only the intervention of several other Iowans prevented the frenzied blacks from slaying Lieutenant John O. Lockhart, the commander of the captured section, and his five remaining gunners. "The negroes want to kill every wounded reb they come to," Chambers added, "and will do it too if we did not watch them."[62]

Throwing his divisions into action piecemeal, Kirby Smith doomed one thousand of his seasoned veterans to death and wounds in a series of fierce but unimaginative frontal assaults against the unyielding Union infantry. Checked and battered, the Confederates drew back to rest and reform and the scene of carnage grew quiet. Steele took advantage of this lull to pull his foot soldiers across the Saline River, leaving the Second Kansas Colored behind to cover the withdrawal of his white regiments. During the two hours that the Second Kansas lingered south of the Saline, Colonel Crawford dispatched details "all along where our lines had stood to pick up such of our wounded as might have been overlooked." A number of black soldiers could not resist the temptation to interrupt their errands of mercy to seek additional revenge for Poison Spring. A few crept as close as they dared to enemy units to fire some farewell shots. Others turned their attention to the wounded Confederates who lay near Union lines.[63]

Hours earlier, a bullet had hit Private John H. Lewis of the Eighteenth Texas Infantry in the leg, rendering him unable to walk. He took shelter behind a tree stump and waited for the battle to play itself out. "After a while the firing ceased," he related, "and our army was gone. Soon I looked around and saw some black negroes cutting our wounded boys' throats, and I thought my time would come next." The adrenalin rush produced by that terrifying discovery restored the use of Lewis's wounded leg, and he limped hurriedly to safety.[64]

Once the Second Kansas Colored finally crossed the Saline River, the Confederates took possession of the battlefield. In numerous spots, they came across evidence of the horrors witnessed by Private Lewis. "The negros killed some of our Wounded," James McCall Dawson of the Thirty-fourth Arkansas Infantry disclosed in a letter home. Assistant Surgeon Junius N. Bragg of the Thirty-third Arkansas Infantry wrote his wife that A.J. Williams, the regiment's acting sergeant major, "had his throat cut by a negro" and lived long enough to tell the tale. David S. Williams, the Thirty-third's senior surgeon and A.J.'s brother, provided more details on this case and those of other atrocity victims: "We found that many of our wounded had been mutilated in many ways. Some with ears cut off, throats cut, knife stabs, etc. My brother…was shot through the body, had his throat cut through the windpipe and lived several days. I saw several who were treated in the same way. One officer…wrote on a bit of paper that his lower jaw and tongue were shot off after the battle was over or during the falling back as referred to above." Another Confederate surgeon, Edward W. Cade of Colonel Horace Randal's Texas brigade, grimly informed his wife: "Our command fell back, and when they again advanced they found several of our wounded who had their throats cut from ear to ear by the Negroes."[65]

*Surgeon William L. Nicholson of the Twenty-ninth Iowa Infantry saw wounded black enlisted men from the Second Kansas Colored Infantry murdered in a field hospital at Jenkins' Ferry and later at the hospital village of Princeton, Arkansas. (Courtesy of the U.S. Army Military History Institute)*

Colonel Crawford marched away from Jenkins' Ferry certain that the reprisals committed by the Second Kansas Colored had taught the Rebels to stop murdering black prisoners. He was wrong. The Federals left 150 soldiers too badly hurt to be moved at an overcrowded field hospital at Jenkins' Ferry. Nine of them were enlisted men from the Second Kansas Colored. Just as the sun began to set, some Confederate cavalry rode up to the hospital and began robbing the Federal dead and wounded. Surgeon William L. Nicholson of the Twenty-ninth Iowa had volunteered to remain with his stricken countrymen, and he later testified: "One [Rebel], dressed as an officer, drew his revolver and shot three wounded 'niggers' who lay in the yard." Nicholson narrowly escaped taking a bullet himself when he loudly protested "this brutal violation of the hospital flag." Two weeks later, the Confederates moved Nicholson and the six surviving Second Kansas men to a more permanent hospital at Princeton, Arkansas. The blacks were quartered in a small storehouse apart from the wounded white Federals. "They had not been long deposited," Nicholson recalled, "when I heard shooting and some one remarked 'The niggers are catching it.'" Glancing at the storeroom, the surgeon saw a Confederate soldier emerge with a smoking revolver in each hand. "I went over at once," Nicholson wrote, "and found all the poor negroes shot through the head."[66]

The heartless events that transpired at Poison Spring, Jenkins' Ferry, and Princeton haunted the participants of the Camden Campaign in the months that followed. Both Union and Confederate soldiers in Arkansas had violated the bounds of civilized warfare, and a sensitive handful feared that the struggle would sink to even deeper levels of savagery. "It looks hard," admitted Private Chambers, "but the rebs cannot blame the negroes when they are guilty of the same trick." Two weeks after Steele returned to Little Rock, one of his officers, Lieutenant William Blain of the Fortieth Iowa Infantry, composed this chilling epitaph for the campaign: "It would not surprise me in the least if this war would ultimately be one of extermination. Its tendencies are in that direction now."[67]

≈

1. Gregory J.W. Urwin, "Notes on the First Confederate Volunteers from Ouachita County, Arkansas, 1861," *Military Collector & Historian* 49 (Summer 1997), 83; J.A. Newman, *The Autobiography of an Old Fashioned Boy* (El Reno, Okla.: privately printed, 1923), 23.

2. Wiley Britton to his wife, "The Camden Expedition," June 1, 1864, p. 10, Wiley Britton Letters, J.N. Heiskell Historical Collection, H-4, 13, UALR Archives and Special Collections, UALR Library, University of Arkansas at Little Rock.

3. John W. Brown, "Diary," April 15, 1865, Arkansas History Commission, Little Rock, Arkansas.

4. Wiley Britton, *The Union Indian Brigade in the Civil War* (Kansas City, Mo.: Franklin Hudson Publishing Co., 1922), 347; U.S. War Department, *The War of the Rebellion: A Compilation of the Official Records of the Union and Confederate Armies*, 128 vols. (Washington, D.C.: Government Printing Office, 1880-1901), series 1, vol. 34, part 1: 657 (hereafter cited as *Official Records*, with all references to series 1, vol. 34, part 1, unless otherwise noted).

5. John M. Harrell, "Arkansas," in Clement A. Evans, ed., *Confederate Military History*, vol. 10 (Seacaucus, N.J.: Blue and Grey, 1975), 239; Virginia Mc'Collum Stinson, "Memories," in Mrs. M.A. Elliott, comp., *The Garden of Memory: Stories of the Civil War as Told by Veterans and Daughters of the Confederacy* (Camden, Ark.: Brown Printing, 1911), 31.

6. Ludwell H. Johnson, *Red River Campaign: Politics and Cotton in the Civil War* (Kent, Ohio: Kent State University Press, 1993), 46-48, 81, 85.

7. *Official Records*, 779-81; Roman J. Zorn, ed., "Campaigning in Southern Arkansas: A Memoir by C.T. Anderson," *Arkansas Historical Quarterly* 8 (Autumn 1949), 241-42; James L. Skinner, III, ed., *The Autobiography of Henry Merrell: Industrial Missionary to the South* (Athens: University of Georgia Press, 1991), 352; Harrell, 238-39; John N. Shepherd, "Autobiography" (Guthrie, Okla., 1908), 42, Richard S. Warner Papers, Tulsa, Oklahoma.

8. *Official Records*, 662, 679-80, 734; Brown, April 15, 1864; Mrs. A.J. Marshall, *Autobiography* (Pine Bluff, Ark.: privately printed, 1897), 101.

9. *Official Records*, 680.

10. *Official Records*, 680, 743, 746-47, 750; Glenn L. Carle, "The First Kansas Colored," *American Heritage*, (February/March 1992), 79-80, 82-90.

11. *Official Records*, 680, 743, 751.

12. Ibid., 743-44.

13. *Official Records*, 743-44, 746, 748-50; Steele's Kansas cavalrymen became notorious for their depredations. For more details on this topic, see Gregory J.W. Urwin, "'We Cannot Treat Negroes...as Prisoners of War': Racial Atrocities and Reprisals in Civil War Arkansas," *Civil War History* 42 (September 1996), 199-200.

14. *Official Records*, 744, 749; Britton, *Union Indian Brigade*, 364.

15. *Official Records*, 790, 819, 825, 828.

16. Ibid., 818-19, 825.

17. Ibid., 818-19, 825-26.

18. *Official Records*, 848-49; Henry Cathey, ed., "Extracts from the Memoirs of William Franklin Avera," *Arkansas Historical Quarterly* 22 (Summer 1963), 102-3;

Stinson, 34; Allan C. Ashcraft, "Confederate Indian Troop Conditions in 1864," *Chronicles of Oklahoma* 41 (Winter 1963-64), 445.

19. *Official Records*, 819, 841, 846.

20. *Official Records*, 791, 819, 826; *Washington (Ark.) Telegraph*, May 11, 1864.

21. *Official Records*, 819.

22. Ibid.

23. Ibid., 744, 751.

24. Ibid., 744, 846.

25. Ibid., 744, 750-52, 755.

26. Ibid., 744, 752, 846-47.

27. William F. Stafford, "Battery Journal," April 18, 1864, M.D. Hutcheson Papers, Camden, Arkansas; Anonymous to "Dear Sally," n.d., Spence Family Collection, Old State House Museum, Little Rock, Arkansas; *Official Records*, 752.

28. *Official Records*, 745, 752.

29. When Colonel Randolph Barnes Marcy, one of the regular army's four inspector generals, inspected the First Kansas Colored on July 19, 1864, he found the regiment armed with "230 U.S. muskets calibre 69 and 126 Enfield rifled muskets calibre 58." Either type could fire buck and ball cartridges. *Official Records*, 745, 752, 847; R.B. Marcy, "Report of Inspection of the Department of Arkansas Made in June and July 1864 by Colonel Randolph B. Marcy, Inspector General U.S. Army," Record Group 94, Office of Inspector General Letters Received, 1863-1876, National Archives, Washington, D.C.

30. Stafford, April 18, 1864; *Official Records*, 792, 818-19, 842; Carle, 79, 82, 84-90.

31. *Official Records*, 745, 752, 847-48.

32. John N. Edwards, *Shelby and His Men; or, The War in the West* (Cincinnati: Miami Printing and Publishing, 1867), 275; *Official Records*, 744, 849; John Hallum, *Reminiscences of the Civil War*, vol. 1 (Little Rock: Tunnah & Pittard, Printers, 1903), 117.

33. *Official Records*, 745, 752.

34. Ibid., 745.

35. Britton, *Union Indian Brigade*, 367; *Official Records*, series 1, vol. 22, part 1: 447-52; Dudley Taylor Cornish, "Kansas Negro Regiments in the Civil War," *Kansas Historical Quarterly* 21 (May 1953), 425.

36. *Official Records*, 752.

37. Ibid., 745, 752.

38. *Official Records*, 745, 754, 757; *Fort Smith New Era*, May 21, 1864.

39. *Official Records*, 828, 842.

40. Ibid., 745, 753.

41. Ibid., 791, 828, 843, 847.

42. Ibid., 753, 755.

43. *Official Records*, 746, 753-54; Anonymous to "Dear Sally," n.d.; Stafford, April 18, 1864; *Fort Smith New Era*, May 7, 1864.

44. *Official Records*, 745-46, 751, 753, 828; Edwards, 275; Charles H. Lothrop, *A History of the First Regiment Iowa Cavalry Veteran Volunteers, From Its Organization in 1861 to Its Muster out of the United States Service in 1866* (Lyons, Iowa: Beers & Eaton,

Printers, 1890), 181; Cathey, 103; "The Federal Occupation of Camden as Set Forth in the Diary of a Union Officer," *Arkansas Historical Quarterly* 9 (Autumn 1950), 215; Skinner, 367.

45. *Official Records*, 746, 748, 749, 756, 757.

46. *Official Records*, 791, 820; *Washington Telegraph*, May 11, 1864; Anonymous to "Dear Sally," n.d.

47. *Fort Smith New Era*, May 7, 14, 21, 1864; *Washington Telegraph*, May 25, 1864.

48. Britton, *Union Indian Brigade*, 372-73; *Official Records*, 847-48; Ralph R. Rea, *Sterling Price: The Lee of the West* (Little Rock: Pioneer Press, 1959), 106; Henry Merrell, "Receipts" Book (Diary), April 18, 1864, Southwest Arkansas Regional Archives, Washington, Arkansas; George Carr to "Dear Father," May 2, 1864, Eugene A. Carr Papers, Archives Branch, U.S. Army Military History Institute, Carlisle Barracks, Pennsylvania; A.W.M. Petty, *A History of the Third Missouri Cavalry: From Its Organization at Palmyra, Missouri, in 1861, up to November Sixth, 1864: With an Appendix and Recapitulation* (Little Rock: J. Wiliam Denby, 1865), 76.

49. *Washington Telegraph*, June 1, 1864.

50. Stafford, April 18, 1864; Zorn, 242-43; Skinner, 367-68.

51. *Washington Telegraph*, May 11, 1864; Lothrop, 182.

52. Urwin, "We Cannot Treat Negroes," 202; *Washington Telegraph*, June 27, 1864, January 13, 1865; *Arkansas Gazette*, November 4, 1853, April 6, June 15, 1855; *Helena Southern Shield*, October 25, December 20, 1856; Skinner, 38-39.

53. *Arkansas Gazette*, October 11, 1862; *Little Rock True Democrat*, April 22, 1863; *Washington Telegraph*, October 15, 1862, June 8, 1864; Anonymous to "Dear Sally," n.d. For a balanced account of the Fort Pillow Massacre, see Brian Steel Wills, *A Battle from the Start: The Life of Nathan Bedford Forrest* (New York: HarperCollins Publishers, 1992), 179-96.

54. *Official Records*, 746, 753-54, 829, 842, 844; *Fort Smith New Era*, May 28, 1864; Stafford, April 18, 1864.

55. According to an anonymous Camden resident, all of the horsemen who accompanied Steele were of poor quality: "The cavalry [of Steele's army] were much inferior generally to the Confederates. Their horses were reduced in flesh very much so." *Washington Telegraph*, May 25, 1864; Edwards, 267, 275; *Official Records*, 753.

56. Steele repeated this blunder on April 23, when he sent a 240-wagon train rolling toward Pine Bluff to pick up more supplies. Desiring a stronger escort, he provided a reinforced brigade—1,200 infantry in three regiments, 240 cavalry, and two artillery sections—but it was not big enough to avert a catastrophe. On April 25, four thousand Rebel cavalry under Brigadier Generals James F. Fagan and Joseph O. Shelby fell on the Union column at Marks' Mills. The Confederates struck in a perfectly coordinated pincers. They made short work of their opponents, capturing thirteen hundred Union soldiers and the entire train. This staggering setback, the second to rock Steele's army within the span of a week, precipitated the Union abandonment of Camden and a desperate retreat to Little Rock. *Official Records*, 712-15, 788-99; F.M. Drake, "Campaign of General Steele," in *War Sketches and Incidents as Related by Companions of the Iowa Commandery of the Loyal Legion of the United States*, vol. 1 (Des Moines: Press of P.C. Kenyon, 1893), 65-66, 68-69; Charles H. Lothrop, "The

Fight at Marks' Mills," n.d., p. 1, Civil War Manuscripts, State Historical Society of Iowa, Des Moines; Ira Don Richards, "The Engagement at Marks' Mills," *Arkansas Historical Quarterly* 19 (Spring 1960), 54-60.

57. *Washington Telegraph*, May 25, 1864; Charles O. Musser to "Dear Father," May 11, 1864, in Barry Popchock, ed., *Soldier Boy: The Civil War Letters of Charles O. Musser, 29th Iowa* (Iowa City: University of Iowa Press, 1995), 127.

58. Samuel J. Crawford, *Kansas in the Sixties* (Chicago: A.C. McClurg, 1911), 117.

59. *Official Records*, 661-68, 781-82, 788-99.

60. *Official Records*, 669-70; Edwin C. Bearss, *Steele's Retreat from Camden and the Battle of Jenkins' Ferry* (Little Rock: Eagle Press, 1990), 102, 161; Crawford, 121-23.

61. *Official Records*, 697-98, 781, 813; *Little Rock Unconditional Union*, May 13, 20, 1864; George Carr to "Dear Father," May 2, 1864; Crawford, 124-28; Lonnie J. White, ed., "A Bluecoat's Account of the Camden Expedition," *Arkansas Historical Quarterly* 24 (Spring 1965), 87-88; William E. McLean, *Forty-Third Regiment of Indiana Volunteers: An Historic Sketch of Its Career and Services* (Terre Haute, Ind.: C.W. Brown, Printer and Binder, 1903), 26; Samuel J. Crawford to Joseph T. Wilson, December 31, 1885, in Joseph T. Wilson, *The Black Phalanx* (Hartford, Conn.: American Publishing Company, 1890), 242; Skinner, 368.

62. Milton P. Chambers to "Dear Brother," May 7, 1864, Milton P. Chambers Papers, Special Collections Division, University of Arkansas Libraries, Fayetteville; *Official Records*, 781, 813; *Little Rock Unconditional Union*, May 20, 1864.

63. Crawford, 131-32; *Official Records*, 759; Samuel J. Crawford to James T. Wilson, December 31, 1885, in Wilson, 245; William L. Nicholson, "The Engagement at Jenkins' Ferry," *Annals of Iowa* 11 (October 1914), 511.

64. Mamie Yeary, comp., *Reminiscences of the Boys in Gray, 1861-1865* (Dallas, Tex.: Smith & Lamar, 1912), 437.

65. James McCall Dawson to "Dear Father Sisters and Brothers," May 5, 1864, in James Reed Eison, ed., "'Stand We in Jeopardy Every Hour': A Confederate Letter, 1864," *Pulaski County Historical Review* 31 (Fall 1993), 52; Junius N. Bragg to Ann Josephine Goodard Bragg, May 5, 1864, in Mrs. T.J. Gaughan, ed., *Letters of a Confederate Surgeon 1861-1865* (Camden, Ark.: privately printed, 1960), 230; Yeary, 799; Edward W. Cade to "My dear Wife," May 6, 1864, Edward W. and Allie Cade Correspondence, John Q. Anderson Collection, Texas State Archives, Austin, Texas.

66. Nicholson, 509, 511-15, 519; *Fort Smith New Era*, June 16, August 6, 1864.

67. Milton P. Chambers to "Dear Brother," May 7, 1864; William Blain to "Dear Wife," May 17, 1864, in Dolly Bottens, comp., *Rouse Stevens Ancestary & Allied Families* (Carthage, Mo.: privately printed, 1970), 108B

# About the Contributors

FRANK AREY is a deputy director with the Department of Arkansas Heritage. He received a B.A. in History from Hendrix College and a J.D. with honors from the University of Arkansas at Little Rock School of Law. He is currently working toward an M.A. in History form the University of Central Arkansas. He is a member of the Company of Military Historians and is an assistant editor of the company's quarterly journal, *Military Collector and Historian*. He is also a member of the Prairie Grove Battlefield Commission.

MARK K. CHRIST is the community outreach director for the Arkansas Historic Preservation Program, an agency of the Department of Arkansas Heritage. In his thirteen years with AHPP, he has been a strong advocate for the preservation of the state's many Civil War battlefields. He developed and instituted the Arkansas Civil War Heritage Trail, a network of regional organizations dedicated to identifying, protecting, interpreting and promoting Arkansas's Civil War-related properties. He served as editor of *Rugged and Sublime: The Civil War in Arkansas*, an overview military history of the war in Arkansas published in 1994 by the University of Arkansas Press, and is the author of *Getting Used to Being Shot At: The Spence Family Civil War Letters*, which was published by the University of Arkansas Press in 2002. He received his bachelor's degree from the University of Arkansas at Little Rock in 1982 and a master of liberal studies with museum emphasis from the University of Oklahoma in May 2000. His thesis developed an interpretive plan for the Union campaign that resulted in the capture of Little Rock in September 1863.

THOMAS A. DEBLACK is an associate professor of history at Arkansas Tech University in Russellville. DeBlack is a member of the Southern Historical Association, the Society of Civil War Historians and the Arkansas Association of College History Teachers, and he sits on the Board of Trustees of the Arkansas Historical Association. He is the co-author of *Rugged and Sublime: The Civil War in Arkansas* and co-editor of *Civil Obedience: An Oral History of School Desegregation in Fayetteville, Arkansas, 1954-1965.* He is currently writing a history of Arkansas in the Civil War and Reconstruction and is one of four authors who developed a college-level Arkansas history textbook.

CARL H. MONEYHON is a professor of history at the University of Arkansas at Little Rock. He has written extensively about Arkansas history during the middle of the nineteenth century. His most recent book is *Arkansas in the New South*, published by the University of Arkansas Press.

RONNIE A. NICHOLS is the owner of Nichols Consulting of Birmingham, Alabama, which provides planning, research, and technical services for documentary films, publications, programs, and exhibits. He is the author of several publications, including "Conspirators or Victims? A Survey of Black Leadership in the Elaine Riots," in the *Arkansas Review: Journal of Delta Studies*, and "A Blend of History, The Third Side of the Civil War: An African-American Perspective," in the *Northeast Mississippi Daily Journal*. The founder of the Arkansas Chapter of the Afro-American Historical and Genealogical Society, he is the former director of the Old State House Museum. He was also a museum evaluator for the Institute of Museum and Library Services for more than ten years. He has a B.A. from the

University of Arkansas at Little Rock and an M.F.A. from the Otis Art Institute of Los Angeles.

GREGORY J.W. URWIN is a professor of history at Temple University in Philadelphia, Pennsylvania, where he is associate director of the Center for the Study of Force and Diplomacy. He is the author or editor of seven books, including *Facing Fearful Odds: The Siege of Wake Island*; *Custer Victorious: The Civil War Battles of General George Armstrong Custer*; and *The United States Infantry: An Illustrated History, 1775-1918*. He is currently editing an essay collection for Southern Illinois Press titled *Black Flag over Dixie: Racial Atrocities and Reprisals in the Civil War*. Urwin's publications have won the General Wallace M. Greene, Jr., Award from the Marine Corps Heritage Foundation and the Harold L. Peterson Award from Eastern National Park and Monument Association. He is also the general editor of the Campaigns and Commanders book series from University of Oklahoma Press.

≈

# Index

**Poison Springs Monument To Be Dedicated September 7**

The monument erected on the Camden Chidester highway by the Daughters of the Confederacy commemorating the battle of Poison Springs, will be unveiled with interesting ceremonies, at 4 o'clock p. m., Sunday, September 7.

To the untiring efforts of Mrs. Dora T. Sifford and the late Nellie D. Tufts, the erection of this monument is largely due.

The following program will be rendered:

Music by Camden Boys Band.
Invocation:    Rev. C. E. Guice.
Song:   Quartet from the Christian church of Camden.
Address:    W. R. Thrasher.
Reading:   Lalla Beth Chidester.
Informal talk by Mrs. C. A. Lathrop, historian for Arkansas division of U. D. C.
Music by Boys Band.
Unveiling of monument.
Benediction:   Rev. H. H. Griffin.

Everybody is invited to be present on this occasion.

*The United Daughters of the Confederacy dedicated a marker at Poison Spring on September 7, 1929. (Courtesy of the Butler Center for Arkansas Studies, Central Arkansas Library System, Little Rock)*